LIBRARY

Understanding Higher Education

An Introduction for Parents, Staff, Employers and Students

Donald Bligh, Harold Thomas &

Ian McNay

intellect™

EXETER, ENGLAND
PORTLAND (OREGON) USA

First Published in 1999 by
Intellect Books
School of Art and Design, Earl Richards Road North, Exeter EX2 6AS

First Published in USA 1999 by
Intellect Books
ISBS, 5804 N.E. Hassalo St, Portland, Oregon 97213-3644

Consulting Editor: Masoud Yazdani
Copy Editor: Lucy Kind
Cover Design: Peter Davies

A catalogue record for this book is available from the British Library

ISBN 1-871516-74-9

Printed and bound in Great Britain by Cromwell Press, Wiltshire

CONTENTS

Foreword

This book could not have been published at a better time. 100,000 more places will become available in higher education between now and 2001/02. Many of these will be filled by students with no previous family experience of higher education or whose family experience dates back to when a small minority of school leavers entered. For them in particular, it is essential that good quality information about higher education exists. This book provides that.

That's not to say I agree with everything in the book. I don't. I do not, for example, share the authors' rather gloomy prediction about future undergraduate demand for higher education. I'm certain that the availability of extra places will stimulate demand. But I do agree that the book provides a fascinating introduction for anyone interested in finding out more about UK higher education as we enter the next century.

I agree wholeheartedly with the authors that increasingly open and clear information about higher education is a must if students are to benefit fully from the extra opportunities now available to them. This book contributes greatly and I hope you enjoy reading it.

Baroness Blackstone
Minister of State for Education and Employment

intellect Books

EDUCATION SERIES – General Editor: Donald Bligh

Seven Decisions when Teaching Students	Donald Bligh, David Jaques and David Warren Piper
Counselling in Study Methods	Mary Wheeler
What's the Use of Lectures?	Donald Bligh
Understanding Higher Education	Donald Bligh, Harold Thomas and Ian McNay
What's the Point in Discussion?	Donald Bligh

Selected Titles on Education Technology

Evaluation of CALL Programs	Keith Cameron (ed)
Computers and English Language Learning	John Higgins
Learning with Computers	Robert Lawler
IT for Learning Enhancement	Moira Monteith
The Virtual Classroom	Starr Roxanne Hiltz
Computers for Educational Administrators	Greg Kearsley

Intellect Books, School of Art and Design, Earl Richards Road North, Exeter EX2 6AS
Tel: 44 (0)1392 475110 Fax: 44 (0)1392 475110
Email: info@www.intellect-net.com

Visit www.intellectbooks.com

Preface

This book is for those people who have not experienced higher education and who now need to know about it. They include parents whose children will benefit from it, employers and employees who will work with students and academics, and foreign students who need to understand the assumptions and culture of British universities.

It is also for academics, parents, teachers, careers advisers and others who have experienced higher education but have never studied higher education itself, or have not kept abreast of the changes. It is particularly suitable for overseas students to understand what they are coming to and what is expected of them. But it is not another guide for intending applicants. The ideas and information brought together in this book will not be found in college prospectuses or university brochures.

The time when children first go to college can be an anxious one for parents. So many things seem uncertain. When the vacation comes the children seem different - they are no longer dependent. Advice is no longer appropriate. That's not surprising. Education is intended to change people.

More understanding is needed. That's why this book is about "Understanding higher education" and the people engaged in it. The Dearing Report and the Government's response to it herald sharp changes in British higher education. When change is rapid we easily forget fundamental principles and things of lasting value. This book presents a reminder.

It is intended as a book for lay men and women, but every vice-chancellor and college principal will find a few things they did not know. It is also intended as background reading for new academic and administrative staff, because, although they may have a good understanding of some aspects of higher education, there will be other aspects of which they have little experience. The same will be true of officers in student unions.

Chapters 2, 3 and 4 form a basis for what follows, but on the whole you can read any chapter independently. So if you just want to dip in here and there, go ahead. You should find that the sub-headings help you.

We have tried to write simply without over simplifying, but some subjects like academic freedom, require a lot of thought no matter how simply they are expressed. Although what we have written is based upon research, for ease of reading we have deliberately not flooded the text with references to the original reports. The book uses data supplied by the Society for Research into Higher Education, by agreement with the Higher Education Statistics Agency. To them, our thanks.

We know some people find statistics difficult. If you are one of them, press on and you should find that the tone of the text will give you the general meaning, even if not its detail.

Much of the text originally appeared as "Higher Education" in the "Education Matters" series under the general editorship of Professor Ted Wragg for whose initiative at that time we are grateful. We are also grateful for encouragement by Profesor Masoud Yazdani and Robin Beecroft of Intellect Books. All chapters have been revised by each of us and updated following the publication of the Dearing Report and the Government's reaction to it. Part of Chapter 3 and Chapters 4 and 11 were the particular responsibility of Harold Thomas; Ian McNay's was Chapters 5, 6, 12 and 14, and mine was Chapters 1, 2, the first part of 3, 7, 8, 9, 10 and 13.

Donald Bligh (Editor)

Glossary

A Level   Advanced Level General Certificate of Education. Examination typically taken at aged 18. Passes in two subjects commonly regarded as minimum entrance qualification for university entrance.

APEL   Accreditation of Prior Experiential Learning.

API   Age Participation Index.

B.Ed   Bachelor of Education. Degree course taken by undergraduates training for the teaching profession.

B.TEC   Business and Technician Education Council.

CATE   Council for the Accreditation of Teacher Education.

CATs   Colleges of Advanced Technology in the post-war period. Set up after the 1056 White paper, "Technical Education". All became universities after the Robbins Report 1963.

CATS   Credit Accumulation Transfer Scheme(s).

CIs   Central Institutions of Scotland. Of similar standing to the Colleges of Education and Polytechnics of England and Wales, but responsible to the Scottish Education Department.

CNAA   Council for National Academic Awards.

CSYS   Certificate of Sixth Year Studies.

CVCP   Committee of Vice Chancellors and Principals.

DfEE   Department for Education and Employment.

EHE   Enterprise in Higher Education.

EU   European Union.

exCATs   Former CATs.

FE   Further Education. Post school education (aged 16+).

GCE   General Certificate of Education. Ordinary Level (O Level) and Advanced Level (A Level) replaced School Certificate Matriculation and Higher School Certificate in 1951.

GCSE   General Certificate of Secondary Education. Examination replacing GCE O Levels, typically taken in schools at aged 16.

GDP   Gross Domestic Product.

GNVQ   General National Vocational Qualification.

HE   higher education.

HEFC   Higher Education Funding Council.

HEFCE   Higher Education Funding Council for England.

HEQC   Higher Education Quality Council.

HESA   Higher Education Statistics Agency.

HND   Higher National Diploma.

ILT   Institute for Learning and Teaching.

IT   Information Technology.

LEAs   Local Education Authorities.

LSE   London School of Economics.

NAB   National Advisory Board for Public Sector Higher Education. See PCFC.

NATFHE   National Association of Teachers in Further and Higher Education.

NVQ4   National Vocational Qualifications Level 4.

O Level   Ordinary Level General Certificate of Education. Established 1951. See GCSE above.

OU   Open University.

PAYE   Pay As You Earn.

PCAS   Polytechnic Central Admissions System. Established 1984. See UCAS.

PCFC   Polytechnics and Colleges Funding Council. Replaced the NAB and replaced by HEFCE.

PhD   Doctor of Philosophy.
PSHE   Public Sector Higher Education.
RAE   Research Assessment Exercise.
SCOTVEC   Scottish Vocational Education Council.
SNVQ   Scottish National Vocational Qualification.
SRHE   Society for Research into Higher Education.
TQA   Teaching Quality Assessment.
UC   University College. eg. University College London.
UCAS   University Central Admissions Service. Merger of UCCA and PCAS 1992.
UCCA   University Central Council for Admissions.
UFC   Universities Funding Council. Replaced UGC. Susseeded by integrated funding bodies for England, Scotland and Wales.
UGC   University Grants Committee.
UK   United Kingdom.
UNESCO   United Nations Educational, Scientific and Cultural Organisation.
USA   United States of America.
UWIST   University of Wales Institute of Science and Technology.

1.   Some Misconceptions

I.   "You get long holidays"

It's early July. "So you'll soon be on holiday until October" shouts my neighbour across the fence. It's a jibe. He says it partly to rile me and partly because he wants to think that dons have a cushy life compared with him. He's a technician. He works in a manufacturing industry with fixed hours of employment.

He doesn't really think that university dons sit around drinking port after lunch, as they are sometimes depicted in television drama, but the visual image from television is very powerful in his mind when there is no other experience to replace it. Besides, he thinks there must be a grain of truth in the television image.

In a way he's left with two conflicting ideas about my job in the back of his mind, because he's never consciously needed to resolve the conflict by discarding one of them.

II.   "You've one job, not two"

If you ask him, he knows perfectly well that people in universities have two jobs, teaching and research, to say nothing of the administration that goes with them. Yet when he thinks of one of them, he ignores the other and thinks it must be full time. So when he thinks of me as a teacher he thinks I have long holidays. When he thinks of me as a researcher he imagines I sit in sublime contemplation and reflection without the commercial pressures and tight deadlines endured by researchers in his company, even though he knows the time I go to work and that I come back in the evening two hours after he's started gardening.

Yet his blind spot is curious. He's a reasonably intelligent man. If he had been born a generation later, he would have gone to university himself. As it is, he goes back indoors and looks at the *News, Tomorrow's World*, science and nature programmes, and other television programmes in which academics speak about their work. He is interested, even enthusiastic, about his company's latest research contract with the University. He is impressed by the advances in modern medicine. He is touched by the care and understanding shown by researchers in child abuse, poverty, dyslexia, and other social and medical problems. Yet, because it's on the box in his living room, he doesn't associate any of this with the institution down the road. It's in a different compartment of his mind.

III.   "Higher education is like school"

There is a gap in his experience. He has been to school and thinks that higher education is like secondary education, only a bit more difficult. What else can he think? He has never had the experience to know anything different. So how could he know what goes on at a university? He confuses education with schooling. Higher education is 'education', so he thinks higher education is a process of receiving instruction from a specialist in the subject. School learning was like that in his day and he sees university teachers as even greater authorities in their subject.

So they probably are. Yet the spirit of enquiry that drives research should make higher education a totally different experience from school. It's a process of searching for the 'truth'. The attitudes towards knowledge and those who profess to know, are quite different. It's an attitude of challenging, testing and criticising the accepted authorities of the day. Knowledge is something that evolves, changes and develops.

Sadly, even today, too many students pass through higher education without understanding how it should be different from school, without challenging their teachers and without knowing much about the research that is going on around them. So perhaps I should not blame my neighbour too much. He's about 60 and regards the students who flood the streets as boisterous 'kids'. He doesn't see the more serious and disciplined side of their lives.

He assumes undergraduate students are between the ages of 18 and 21 because he thinks they mostly come straight from school at the age of 18. That's no longer true. The picture is changing fast. According to Dearing, in 1988 13.6% of full-time university students were over 21 when they entered. With the expansion of student numbers that figure in 1996 was 24%, and another 19% reached 21 during their first year. In 1988 7% were over 25; in 1997, 17%. If part-time entrants are included 48% of new students were over 21 in 1997 and 39% were over 25. In fact 79% of part-time entrants were over 25. Before starting their course some students broaden their experience by travel abroad. Others (45%) were employed, including 3% looking after children. So the idea that students have no experience of the world outside school is a mistaken generalisation.

IV.   "Students are irresponsible libertines"

And there's another thing my neighbour doesn't understand. When at school, children are dependent upon their teachers and parents. Higher education cultivates independence of mind. Students must learn to think for themselves. I am quite delighted when I see my students marching in protest at something, organising a Rag for charity, or going on a sponsored walk. Whether I agree with their protest, or whether they support my favourite charity is unimportant. At least they care. Far from being irresponsible, they are taking responsibility where many of us have given up. They are not apathetic. They are thinking for themselves. They are challenging those of us in positions of influence to justify what we do and think. If they can't be enthusiastic when they're young, what are they going to be like when they have to be respectable in middle age? In fact my concern is the opposite:- pressures upon students' time, their need for supplementary incomes, and their fear of the 'authorities' make students less willing to take to the streets.

Higher education is the first opportunity many students have had to explore and work out their own values, in particular those concerned with religion, politics and personal relationships. It's the first time they are free from the constraints of home and school. For many students the most important thing they take away from college is a clearer understanding of themselves and the principles by which they will live.

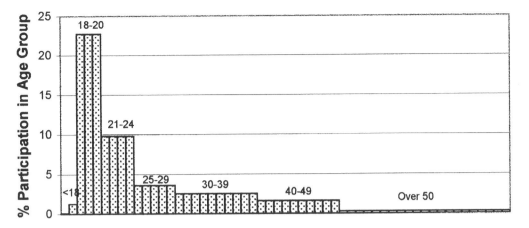

Age Group

Figure 1.1   Participation in higher education by selected age groups.
Source: Dearing Report.

My neighbour doesn't exactly have an image of students going to bed with each other in rotation. But he thinks their new found freedom often leads to behaviour that is over licentious. He is quite mistaken. Considering their time of life and the close community life that they lead, students are a particularly responsible group. (Try comparing them with businessmen or politicians!) But even supposing my neighbour is not entirely mistaken, if you don't hold a dogmatic view about what is right and wrong for yourself and everyone else, you should allow students some leeway to explore these issues for themselves. It would be hypocritical if college authorities said to their students, 'You should come to college to learn to think for yourself and to seek the truth in an open-minded and honest way; but we insist that your truth and your morality should be the same as ours.'

My neighbour doesn't understand why I not only tolerate, but even encourage, students to explore opinions and beliefs I do not myself hold, and may not even understand. He's a bit of a dogmatist. He went to a school where the rules were laid down, principally by the headmaster. Facts and morals were given a spurious and dogmatic certainty. Punishment followed violation. It was the same when he was in the army. His company also operates with very definite rules and procedures. In the same way he applies the principles of engineering as a set of certainties in his work. He doesn't have a mind that is constantly seeking new ways to do things.

Consequently he has difficulty in imagining how a university community could operate where, not only are these things accepted as uncertain, open to doubt, scrutiny and change, but where uncertainty, doubt and scrutiny are actively fostered by those in positions of influence. His whole life experience would render him uncomfortable in such a climate. It's hardly surprising that he's socially conservative and disapproves of students who break the conventions to which he has long been accustomed.

The truth is that higher education is at the forefront of change. Men and women live by their ideas, and those ideas change the world. But change is threatening. It threatens those in power and it threatens those who have to change with it. Because change produces uncertainty and uncertainty makes us feel insecure, there are established powerful forces that will not welcome the products of higher education, particularly those ideas that challenge established values. To my neighbour science and engineering are acceptable. He can use them without being disturbed in himself. But a challenge to change his values is another matter, not least because he, himself, is not equipped to study them.

V.   "It's all theory, not practical"
The very fact that my neighbour is unsettled by a challenge to his values shows that the challenge is a very practical one. It's so practical that my neighbour wants to avoid it by saying 'It's all irrelevant and theoretical'.

The challenge is part of the democratic process. It's a process of evolution. Higher education is part of that process. Education is necessarily political. Politics is the use of power by taking decisions. The decisions depend upon knowledge, ideas and the capacity to think using them. These things are acquired in higher education. That is why universities have long been the seedbed of politics. But my neighbour thinks that education, politics, and religion should somehow be kept in separate watertight compartments. In some European countries the links are much stronger. He underestimates how far all knowledge is interconnected. You can't separate these things. It's strange he should think that, because he also thinks everything we teach should be practical and relevant to modern life. But as soon as the students in history and sociology start relating what they've learned to the contemporary world, he thinks they should get off the streets and get back to their books. He was taught history as a series of facts, not as a series of decisions raising fundamental principles and not as an appreciation of how other people think.

He contrasts theory and practice. In the back of his mind are sentences like 'That's all very well in theory, but it won't work in practice'. The contrast is a mistake. There are good theories and bad theories. And good theories are very practical. He doesn't think of new designs for his company's product as speculations or hypotheses; but, until they are tested in practice, they are just as hypothetical as models in university economics or engineering departments.

He thinks that, just as many of his former colleagues were with his company man and boy, academics have always been academics and have no practical experience outside an ivory tower. He's quite wrong. Depending on the subject, academics typically average six to ten years experience in industry, commerce or the professions before entering academia. Indeed, if they averaged much more than that in a rapidly changing world, colleges could be accused of appointing staff who are out of date, past their most creative years, and form a generation gap with their younger students. More than that, many academics work as consultants and researchers in partnership with other employers. Many courses involve visiting lecturers from varied areas of employment. Others include work placements with placement supervisors engaged in tutoring and assessment.

So the idea that there are barriers between universities and other areas of employment is quite mistaken. Indeed employers probably have more cross-fertilisation of experience with universities than they do with other areas of employment.

VI. "Higher education sponges on the taxpayer"

My neighbour thinks that higher education sponges on the taxpayer. He has a simple argument: 'All the nation's wealth comes from those who make things and sell them, namely from agriculture and manufacturing industry. Services, like education, are financed either from Income Tax, V.A.T. or other taxes on those who produce things. People in industry and agriculture don't owe educationalists a living.' He resents students' grants and thinks parents should pay. It's an argument used by Keith Joseph when he was Minister of Education in the Thatcher Government and again now with the introduction of parental fees. The short answer to the last point is that parents, the students themselves, or someone, always have paid something; but my neighbour's misconception is more fundamental.

It is of course true that all economic activities are ultimately dependent upon primary production. But it doesn't follow from that, that service industries and other activities make no contribution to the economy. Quite the contrary, the service sector in the UK earns far more foreign business than primary production and that includes foreign contracts with universities. In addition the location of new enterprises in Britain shows how universities attract foreign investment. Furthermore, the enormous advances in agriculture and industry have been dependent upon research and inventions in institutions of higher education. My neighbour will deny that by pointing out, quite rightly, that his company employs researchers of its own. But he underrates how far those researchers obtained their skills in the education system. Furthermore, they use knowledge from basic research that no company would ever have sponsored. The fundamentals of laser technology were discovered by a physicist playing with basic ideas. He did not sit down and say 'Now I am going to invent laser technology'. Advances in fundamental knowledge are not made like that.

My neighbour underestimates another aspect of how advances in knowledge are made. He underestimates their inter-disciplinary nature. Companies don't employ researchers in a wide range of disciplines on the off-chance that they will cross-fertilise each other to produce ideas that might be relevant to their particular product. It would be foolish for hundreds of thousands of companies to employ researchers in fields not obviously relevant to their work just hoping that they might interact creatively in a way that happens to be useful. It would be inappropriate for companies to act independently in this way. What is needed is a number of institutions where researchers from a wide range of disciplines can work together, exchanging ideas and building up a resource of knowledge, available nationally when it is needed. In other words, industry and the nation require inter-disciplinary research institutions.

That is precisely what universities are. If we didn't have them, we would have to re-invent them. It would be inefficient to do research any other way. Yet there was a widespread belief in industry that universities were inefficient (until the Jarratt Committee said the universities they looked at were 'well managed'. See Chapter 4).

VII.   Only students and their parents benefit from higher education

Institutions of higher education are national resources of knowledge. (They are not the only ones. Libraries, museums and, increasingly, databases also store knowledge for use when needed.) So it would be quite wrong to suppose that students, their parents or their spouses are the only people who benefit from higher education. The same is true of school education. It would be foolish to suggest that only parents benefit from their children being able to read and write. The whole of our society is organised on the assumption that most people can. Our levels of literacy are a national resource. That is why governments are concerned about it. It is knowledge in people's minds that can be used. The same is true of the knowledge, ideas and thinking skills bestowed by higher education.

It would therefore be quite wrong to suggest that students or their parents alone should pay for higher education. Everyone would be poorer without it. The nation should pay to ensure that those who can acquire the skills demanded by higher education and employers should do so. That way we can all benefit. The intelligence of our young people is a national resource, not merely a personal one, and it is the nation that should invest in it. It is therefore quite right that the taxpayer should do so.

VIII.   So what's higher education really like?

Actually my neighbour never asks this question. I'm glad about that, because it would take some time to tell him over the garden fence. I would have to tell him what is in this book. I would have to tell him that higher education has several different purposes (Chapter 2). Sometimes they're incompatible.

Like his company, higher education is the way it is (Chapter 4), because of its history (Chapter 3). But, unlike his company, it's got a mighty long history and many of the factors that influenced that history are abstract ideas.

The students we get also influence what higher education is like (Chapters 5 and 6). So do the methods of teaching and learning, research and assessment (Chapters 7, 8 and 9). Unlike employees in other walks of life, there are special circumstances in which academics claim the freedom not always to do what their employer wants. This is explained in Chapter 10. Nonetheless, as in any other organisation, the management, finance and staff of universities (Chapters 11, 12 and 13) have a major influence on their character. Finally, like other spheres of work, higher education is constantly changing; so we must peep into the future (Chapter 14).

We'll look at each of these in turn, but the chapters don't have to be read in that order. You can dip in more or less where you like. If you don't understand something because we dealt with it in an earlier chapter, the Contents and the Index will tell you where to find it explained.

2. What is Higher Education For?

Higher education benefits its students and the community as a whole. For both it develops what psychologists call affect:- attitudes, emotions, motivation, values and interpersonal skills based upon feelings for others. It develops cognition:- knowledge, perception and thought. And it develops adaptable occupational skills by the application of cognition and affect. This gives six inter-connected aims of higher education as shown in the Figure 2.1 below. Do these aims conflict? What are the priorities? Let's consider each in turn.

I. To develop attitudes and emotional integrity

Education is primarily about emotions. Imagine your child has Down's syndrome, spina bifida or some other disability. Your main concern won't be that he should go to university, or get a degree, or even that he will be able to live a normal life. Your most important aim will be that he will have a happy life even if it is not a very long one. Happiness is a collection of emotions.

When the chips are down, what is most important in life is survival and security; to love and be loved; to trust and be trusted; to have self-esteem and the esteem of others; to have self-confidence and to impart it; and to be honest, hard-working and responsible. These things have more to do with the emotions than the intellect, more to do with feelings than thoughts, more to do with attitudes than knowledge. Milgram was asked to study why apparently decent middle-class young men could stab a Vietnamese baby 20 times. He found that these young men had experienced fear and obedience to authority in their childhood and adolescence. Their motivation emerged from repressed aggression, punishments and the emotional stresses that they suffered as children. The same was true of ordinary citizens in Germany and Austria before the Second World War, yet no one recognised it. There are similar repressions in our own

Figure 2.1 *The aims of higher education.*

	Individual students	**Community**
Affect	I Attitudes, Values, Emotional Integrity, Interpersonal skills	IV Cultural development
Cognition	II Knowledge and Skills of thinking	V Knowledge and research As a national resource
Adaptable Occupational Skills	III Employment	VI Adaptable highly trained Work force

society, not least where there is neglect or excessive discipline at home or at school, or where there is discrimination or poverty in our inner cities.

A warm, caring and stable environment during early childhood normally produces a well adjusted, sociable adult with interpersonal skills; fear results in either low self confidence or aggression. Yet school league tables not only ignore these priorities, they militate against them. Tests of academic performance as at present designed for 7, 11 and 14 year-olds, pressure teachers to use a didactic authoritarian style and to neglect the education of the emotions.

Authoritarian attitudes breed intolerance. That is inimical to higher education, to harmony in the work place and to a happy marriage. The more we know about the emotional development of children and young people, the more important the earliest years of childhood appear to be. Yet there is little on parenthood in the national curricula.

These defects in school education must affect the aims of higher education. Colleges cannot assume that they are recruiting well-rounded, well-adjusted individuals. To compensate, the education of attitudes, values and emotions must become a major aim of higher education.

This aim is not new. Higher education has always been concerned with attitudes and values. These attitudes include a commitment to consider the moral implications of different findings and practices; taking responsibility for one's own life-long learning; and a passionate commitment to seek the truth in a calm rational impartial dispassionate manner. They necessitate discussion, tolerance towards those who have formed a different opinion, and a willingness to listen to others with an open mind.

II.   To cultivate the intellect

By cultivating the intellect I mean developing knowledge and the capacity to think. In higher education it is the capacity to think that is the more important of these two.

It is not the quantity of knowledge, or what the knowledge is of, that gives knowledge its quality. It is the way that knowledge is learned, related, justified and applied that is important. It is the method that matters. It is a matter of attitudes and abilities in thinking. What you think about is less important than the quality of thought. Thinking includes solving problems, taking decisions, exercising judgement, and being creative. These skills involve applying principles, analysing complex situations, relating disparate knowledge, re-interpreting facts, and the rigorous use of evidence and reasoned argument to reach a conclusion.

What distinguishes a student with highly educated attitudes and intellect from one who only knows a lot about his subject? That was the question tackled by Cardinal Newman in lectures on the founding of Catholic colleges in Ireland in 1852. The resulting book, "The idea of a university", has become a classic. Although almost no one today would think, as he did, that the cultivation of the intellect should be the only aim of a university, few people would deny its importance.

Newman would say, thus educated, students will value the truth. They will challenge their roots and rethink the influences of their parents and school. They will exercise judgment that takes years to acquire and will know when judgement should be resisted or withheld. They will be as consistent as possible and aware of their inconsistencies. They will avoid prejudice, discern irrelevance, appreciate implications, restrain their emotions, remove their ignorance and give only due weight to their preoccupations. They will proceed from the known to the unknown and will recognise 'whereof they cannot speak'.

The one word which sums this up is "criticism". I don't mean only negative criticism. I mean the capacity to make a reasoned judgement.

At one time it was believed that if you get the quality of intellect right, you will be able to apply it to anything. You will be a Master of Arts, able to master any art or occupation. I don't think many people believe that now. Nevertheless, the associated belief that what one knows is less important than the quality of one's thinking, that knowledge is less important than intellect, still has a lot of credibility. And employers demonstrate that credibility annually, not only by preferring graduates to non-graduates, but by preferring graduates from institutions with a reputation for training critical minds, to those perceived as focussing upon knowledge.

III.   Employment

As the last section indicates, if students can achieve aims I and II, they have a better chance of finding employment than those who can't. As the Government's Dearing Inquiry into Higher Education put it in 1997, "The essence of professionalism is
*   a thorough and up to date grasp of the fundamental knowledge base of an occupation;
*   sufficient understanding of the underlying theoretical principles to be able to adapt to novel circumstances and to incorporate research findings into practice; and
*   appropriate practical skills and professional values."

IV.   To develop culture and standards of citizenship

This is what the Dearing Inquiry into Higher Education called "Shaping a democratic and civilised society". It is concerned with contributing to the moral conscience of the nation and with behaviour at leisure, at home and at work.

The Inquiry points out that ours is a multi-cultural society and we need to live together in a harmonious democracy. Democracy is part of our culture. Our democracy and culture increasingly assume that people can make sophisticated judgements and that research findings are available for them to do so. Judgements and research are the stuff of higher education.

Democracy is not just a set of rights. It includes organisations and individuals taking responsibility for their actions, for sharing knowledge, for appreciating how their own arguments and actions will be perceived by others, and caring for minorities and the weak, as well as for the will of the majority.

This aim is concerned with the ability to see things in different ways and to exercise balanced judgement in the light of those varied perceptions. It is concerned with the ability to see many different sides to a question, to understand different points of view, to value diverse objects and activities, and to appreciate cultures, nations and groups other than one's own. This requires having many different concepts which can be used to interpret any situation. Higher education aims to develop those concepts.

Hence cultured people have social skills and breadth of understanding. For this reason, they exhibit tolerance of others who may see things differently. Tolerance is a mark of an educated society. Thus standards of citizenship embody not only skills of perception and judgement, but a number of attitudes. Citizenship includes promoting greater equality in social and economic opportunities. It involves contributing to the educational and general well-being of the community through the application of knowledge and the encouragement of creativity.

This aim might be criticised as vague, but some vagueness is inevitable because it emphasises breadth. As soon as concepts like culture and citizenship are made precise, their meaning becomes limited and that is just the opposite of what is intended.

It can also be misunderstood in two other ways. One is that a cultured person is someone who appreciates specific elitist kinds of art, engages in affluent leisure activities and can communicate effectively. Secondly, it is too often forgotten that science and engineering are a major aspects of our culture. The idea that science and engineering students need a dollop of humanities in order to be cultured, but that humanities students don't need to appreciate science or engineering, is a travesty of higher education. The early specialisation and over-specialisation in our educational system too often gives knowledge to the leaders of tomorrow, at the expense of the values that foster wisdom.

V.   Knowledge and research as a national resource

Human beings think they are the most powerful and most important creatures on earth. I sometimes think that whales and certain viruses might also claim this honour. The case in favour of human beings must rest, not only upon their capacity to think, but upon their accumulation of knowledge. The human race survives and dominates in its environment through the use of knowledge. This is our potential asset and that fact is the reason why we should develop it to the maximum.

If developing knowledge is so important, we should make sure we hang on to what we've got (and that means developing libraries of books, video tapes and computerised databases) and we should train people to get new knowledge that is reasonably certain and will stand the test of time. That is the process of doing research and training researchers that takes place in higher education. In many fields, the frontiers of new knowledge are very distant from ordinary people now. That is why training of the best minds is necessary. So training the best minds for research is fundamental to the development of the human race. If we didn't have universities that did so, it would be best to invent them.

Universities are the major institutions in our society for the acquisition, preservation, assembly, classification, interrelation, testing, interpretation and dissemination of knowledge, particularly new knowledge. They therefore have a major role in the advancement of our society.

There is an objection to that argument. Can't industry, the professions and other occupational groups, carry out all the research that is necessary without having special institutions for the job?

There are several answers to this objection. Firstly, it has been estimated that about 20% of the research done in Britain is indeed done in the private sector. Other estimates put the figure much higher. One puts it as high as 65% including one-third of Government research contracted out. In practice, we don't really know how much is going on, and that is one of the difficulties. If no one else knows about the research that is being carried out, it is hardly making a long term contribution to the pool of knowledge in books, on tapes and in databases.

Secondly, until recently, Government sources estimated that about half the research in Britain was being carried out by, or for, the Ministry of Defence and was more likely to obliterate the human race than help it master its environment. Higher education was funded directly for about 10% of the research in Britain, but it gets money for another 10% or more through research contracts. Universities get research contracts when industry and the Government recognise that universities are in a better position to do it. For example, higher education employs people whose job is not only to keep up-to-date on the latest knowledge in specialist areas, but also to rub shoulders with people who are up-to-date in other areas of knowledge so that cross-fertilisation can take place. The private sector rarely has this advantage. Smaller companies cannot afford to employ full-time permanent researchers. It is much cheaper for them to employ a research organisation when they need it. Universities are such organisations. Furthermore the private sector cannot afford to undertake fundamental research or pursue knowledge in a disinterested manner.

Higher education is most important in carrying out fundamental research. This research often seems remote from application, yet it is fundamental to other research developments. Yet because it is fundamental, it is essential to a very wide range of later developments. Essential research that cannot be paid for by the private sector must be paid for by the public purse.

It is for this reason Research Councils were established. Tragically, governments have little short-term incentive to encourage the Research Councils to support fundamental research which will not be applied within the lifetime of that government. With fluctuations in funding, the existence of permanent institutions to maintain the capacity to do fundamental research is important in counteracting the short term interests of governments. In short, all these are reasons for having specialist institutions concerned with developing, and exploiting to the maximum, our major resource - our brains.

VI.   To provide an adaptable workforce with a broad range of skills

Since the Second World War the view of successive governments has been very simple. The nation's economy needs trained personnel. It is industry that will improve the economy. So we must improve the training of people for industry. Industry needs scientists and engineers. So let's have more science and engineering students and fewer people studying the arts.

'But why do you want the nation to be more wealthy?', I ask. *Don't be silly'*, I hear you say, *'Everyone wants more money.'* 'Why?', I insist.

'Well if you've got surplus money after you've bought the necessities of life, you can buy luxuries and entertainment and other things that lead to a happy, contented and enjoyable life.'

'So what you really want is a happy, contented and enjoyable life. Having money is not the only path to happiness and contentment. In fact people with a lot of money are not always the most contented. In any case, if that's what you want, why don't we educate people so that they can be happy, contented and enjoy themselves by other means as well as spending money? For example, humans are essentially social animals. Much, if not most, happiness, contentment and enjoyment comes from having good relationships with other people. Shouldn't we educate people about relationships? The social sciences, management and literature all have a role here. In which case it's not only science and engineering that are important. A great deal of enjoyment can also be obtained if we educate people to appreciate the arts, like music. That means we must train people to perform and produce artistic works. So perhaps we should make sure our higher education system trains people in the arts as well as science, engineering and the social sciences.'

'OK, I accept that we don't only want to train scientists and engineers. Indeed we need doctors, lawyers, teachers and a lot of other professions you haven't mentioned. The question is, `How many of each?' It's a question of getting the right balance. It ought to be possible to work out how many we need of each and educate the right number.'

'That used to be called manpower planning. The Government tried it in the 1970s, but it doesn't work except in a very rough and ready way. We know we need more doctors than pharmacists, but we don't know how many. There are a lot of reasons why we can't forecast the numbers needed with acceptable accuracy.

  'First it takes many years to train a doctor and quite a few to train a pharmacist, a lawyer, a teacher, an engineer or any other graduate. Courses have to be designed, validated and often accredited by the professions before a college can even begin to advertise for applicants. Students start applying at least a year before they enter the course. So the time lag between designing a three-year course and students getting jobs having taken it, is likely to be four and a half years at the very least. Now imagine a company trying to forecast its labour requirements for 4 or 5 years' time! It's quite impractical. Admittedly the attraction of one-year postgraduate professional courses is that they ease this problem a bit; but many jobs can't be learned in nine months, particularly as the world becomes more complicated.

  'Second, changing economic conditions affect demand. So do changes in technology.

  'Third, people do not stay in a job for a lifetime or even enter the one they trained for. So we don't know how many graduates we have already trained will move out leaving a vacancy. Furthermore specific job skills do not last a lifetime. But we cannot know for every conceivable skill how long a graduate will retain it. Nor do we know, when graduates will become out-of-date, whether they will retrain, leave their professions, or do nothing about it.

'Fourth, we don't know how many women will return to work in any profession after having children, or how long they will wait to do so. Some return when their children start school. Some return much earlier, some much later and some never at all.

'Fifth, we cannot forecast the emigration and immigration for particular professions. The labour market is international now, particularly in Europe and amongst graduates.

'Finally, the assumptions about the traditional age of retirement are no longer valid. In short, although accurate forecasts might be desirable, neither the Government, the professional bodies nor the universities can make useful predictions of the number of graduates who will be needed in any specific profession in four or five years' time.'

'If planning is no good, we should be able to achieve the right balance of occupational skills by letting free market forces operate. If the country needs more scientists and engineers they will be paid more, and then more school children will opt to do these subjects.'

That doesn't work either. The market that operates is the more immediate one, the higher education market, not the job market. The country has been short of scientists and technicians for 50 years. Although 65% of all students in a recent small survey gave getting a job or qualification as their most important reason for entering higher education, once they had arrived they wanted to develop new or existing skills (86%), to broaden horizons (80%), to enjoy intellectual growth and stimulation (79%), to meet new people (73%), new ideas (71%) and to increase self-esteem and confidence (63%).

Most school children don't enter higher education because of the money they might get. In one piece of research, school leavers rated "Interest in my subject" at an average of 3.9 on a scale between 0 and 5. Average ratings for "Obtaining a general education" and "Furthering my career" were 3.5 and 3.4 respectively. All other reasons were rated 1.6 or lower.

Furthermore if the job market was influential, the same time lag problem would apply. The response to demand would only take effect 5 years later when conditions might have changed. Indeed, most pupils begin to show a preference for Arts or Science around the age of 13 and many have to make curricular commitments around that age. As graduates, they only reach the job market about nine years later.

In any case students' choice of career at this stage is more influenced by what they think they would enjoy doing - that is expected job satisfaction - than by expectations of high financial rewards. A survey has shown that most school leavers do not have monetarist values. In any case, although children have a general knowledge of what is well paid, it is doubtful how effectively detailed information about salaries and job opportunities penetrates the schools. Admittedly this is changing. There is reason to think that the introduction of course fees and higher education loans have made job security more important.

However, I didn't say planning is no good at all; only that detailed manpower planning for specific jobs doesn't work. The less specific the prediction demanded, the more plausible manpower planning becomes. This is partly because, when people change jobs, they are more likely to change to one in the same broad category, than in the same narrow one.

All this means that it is a mistake for governments and employers to think higher education should provide specific job skills. The aim should be "To provide an adaptable highly trained work force with a broad range of occupational skills". The education should be in general, not specific, occupational skills.

There are educational reasons, too, why we should not always train our graduates for specific jobs. Jobs require specific mental skills based upon a combination of sub-skills with much wider application. If you teach the sub-skills separately the job may take longer to learn, but the students will not only do the job better because they will have better understanding of it, but they will also be able to apply the sub-skills to other areas of work.

To keep it simple, let me take an example from every day life outside the world of higher education. Staff at a cash desk in a supermarket can be trained to register the price of each separate purchase, press a button to add them up, type in the sum of money proffered, and get the machine to work out the change required. They don't need any powers of arithmetic. But if they had some knowledge of arithmetic, they would be able to *understand* what they are doing and know if they got it wrong. They would also be able to answer customers' queries because they would be able to *exercise critical judgement* of whether they had done it correctly. They would not be automata pushing buttons. Learning arithmetic would take longer, but it could be *applied* to other areas of life and, could possibly be used in other paid employment.

"Understanding", "application" and "exercising critical judgement" are important educational aims of higher education too. They are based upon a knowledge of the principles involved. Principles are generalisations. Much of higher education consists of learning, testing and applying generalisations. Generalisations are necessary in any job where the circumstances for action are not always the same - in other words, where there is complexity. Consider radiographers. If they tried to learn how to take an X-ray of the wrist, the leg, the chest and so on, all as separate tasks, they would never get to the end of the list; and if they did, they would not do their job very well because every patient is different. They need to know generalisations about anatomy, radiation physics, etc. and to know how to apply them to a multitude of different cases. Yet even a radiographer's cognitive skills are simple compared with that of a personnel manager, an accountant, a teacher, or an engineer.

So "To provide an adaptable highly trained work force with a broad range of occupational skills" is a much more plausible aim for higher education than any aim that is job-specific. This conclusion can be supported by an economic, as well as an educational, argument. Companies are increasingly international. They choose where to build their factories and establish new business. A large potential labour force with a broad base of adaptable occupational skills is a major attraction, if not essential. The nation cannot afford to turn business away by neglecting this aim of higher education.

VII. Aims from other perspectives

As I've said, much of higher education is about exploring questions from many different perspectives. That is just what we've been doing in this chapter.

Section I is particularly from a parent's perspective, although employers and many others are also concerned about the attitudes and emotional welfare of new graduates.

Section II is more concerned with developing the individual's thinking, while Section III is from the perspective of the individual's career and financial prospects.

Section IV is about the community and organisations in which graduates will live and work. It has a social perspective.

Section V is about the growth of knowledge for posterity and the human race.

And Section VI is more from the perspective of the Government.

These perspectives don't usually conflict, but they could do. There are also many other perspectives that could be taken. Some of them are a mixture of the six perspectives already taken. For example one perspective could be administrative: universities provide experts. The experts may be consultants or critics. As consultants, academics are used by the Government, the Civil Service, industry and commerce. As a source of informed criticism of government, universities have a constitutional role and can be viewed from that perspective. Academic work can also be seen from the standpoint of its effect upon the environment, upon world health, upon poverty and upon international relations. Researchers can be seen as an international community with common interests, values and channels of communication through the Internet. Higher education is an agent of change; and that is another perspective. No doubt there are many more that could be added.

The important point is that no one perspective should exclude the others. Diversity is desirable in higher education. It produces a creative tension because each perspective emphasises some values more than others. Single-mindedness is inimical to higher education. For this reason its values, and hence its whole style of organisation, are quite different from many undertakings in industry and commerce.

Further Reading

National Committee of Enquiry into Higher Education (1997), 'Aims and Purposes' (Chapter 5) in *Higher Education in the Learning Society The Report of the National Committee (The Dearing Report)*, pp 70-86.

3.   How the System Developed

The heritage
I.   The principles of higher education come from ancient Athens

Western civilisation has evolved from three earlier cultures. From Galilee it obtained its religion, many of its moral principles, its national and domestic rituals, its community focus, the stability of the family and its softer values including its service to those it loves, its care for those that suffer, its compassion for the weak and its concern for the needy. From Rome it inherited the basis of its laws, the foundations of its government, its separation of judiciary and executive, the rigour of its organisation, its repression of human feelings and its use of military power. From Athens it acquired its desire for knowledge, its scientific quest, its pursuit of arts and its canons of criticism.

Their legacies in Britain are represented by the Church, the State and the universities. Yet each is concerned with the affairs of the others. None has been exclusively concerned with the power of the spirit, the power of government or the powers of the mind. Nor has any exclusively valued the soul, material wealth or ideas. Yet each has had some constitutional independence. Consequently they exist in a mutual tension, each keeping the excesses of the others in check. In different phases of history one has dominated the others or a coalition has prevailed upon the third. It is easy to think of the Middle Ages as when the Church had more temporal and educational power than today; whilst in the past 20 years the Government has increasingly obliged the universities to serve its will.

It may seem harder to think of a time when the universities dominated the Church and State; but that is because we tend to think of power in terms of political, administrative, legal or military power - the values of Rome, not the values of Athens. The powers of the mind are altogether more indirect and general. The effects of education are not immediate, but they last a lifetime and pervade everything a person does. That is power indeed.

Their influence is enormous. Stand back and look at British universities objectively. They are remarkably successful institutions. Some have lasted 700 years. None has ever closed (though there have been two mergers). All have expanded. They have educated the leaders in politics, administration, the professions and most other walks of life. And, of course, the whole educational system, through which nearly everyone now passes, is strongly influenced in its curricula, its examinations, its organisation, its inspectorate and its teachers by ways of thinking disseminated from higher education.

Yet what is important in the legacy from Athens is not an institution. (The first universities, as we know them, were not established at Bologna and Paris until the 12th century, nearly 1,800 years later.) Nor was the legacy a body of knowledge. (What is regarded as certain knowledge in one period, is often shown to be mistaken or meaningless in another.)

The important legacy is the method of advancing knowledge. Instead of propounding his beliefs, Socrates asked questions. In his case they were usually philosophical questions, such as what we mean by "justice", "friendship" or "reality"; but the subject matter is irrelevant. Socrates's method was to probe the answers given with more questions, thereby taking his students ever deeper into the subject. He often showed that their common sense beliefs were inconsistent, or conflicted, with other evidence. Whilst his students learned about the subject, they also learned what they did not, and could not, know. They learned about themselves.

This method is still central to university teaching and research today, and it brings the two together as part of the same activity - the quest for understanding by criticism of ideas. It has the following crucial features. A recognition that: - no belief is so sacred that it cannot be challenged; - knowledge is tentative, not fixed and static. It is constantly being discarded or reshaped, created or reinvented, discovered and expanded. Learning is a research activity, a voyage of discovery. The voyage progresses by ideas being subjected to critical tests, in particular, common observation and the impartiality of reason, not the authority of individuals or organisations, whatever their position or wealth. Discussion is an essential process. Asking and anticipating questions, penetrating questions, is an essential skill. The most effective teaching consists of pulling ideas out of students, not drumming them in. And there should not only be tolerance of those who hold opinions that threaten one's own, but active co-operation in assisting them to pursue their truth wherever it may lead.

The process of questioning includes challenging the answers given by authorities, whether those authorities be the Government, the Church, teachers, experts, those with experience, employers or parents. If you cannot understand this questioning attitude, you cannot understand what distinguishes higher education from other areas of learning. The persistent challenging of those with authority creates a tension in our society that is innovative and constantly adapting to change. Without that constant challenge, our society will be static, out-of-date, backward and miserable. That is why "Britain needs its universities", why students ought to be radical - that is to rethink the fundamentals of everything, and why they are at a time of life when some rebellion is to be understood and encouraged.

Athens produced Aristotle, probably the greatest intellect who ever lived. He is thought to have written over 400 volumes. His work on logic stood unrivalled until just over 100 years ago. His books on ethics and metaphysics are still studied today. He also wrote, albeit less convincingly to modern eyes, on astronomy, physics, mathematics, geology, politics, marriage, education, psychology, and art. Many of the basic concepts of science came from his mind. He was tutor to Alexander The Great. Above all, he was a naturalist. Species are still being rediscovered that he had dissected and described. (You may think he did all this without a research grant. You would be wrong! Alexander's soldiers brought back specimens and documents galore. Someone has estimated that the cost would be the equivalent of over £250M in modern currency.)

II.   Medieval knowledge came from authorities and contested discussion

Yet in a way, the forerunners of the medieval university, Plato's "Academy" and Aristotle's "Lyceum", were almost too successful. For a very long time afterwards, ordinary mortals felt there was no point in going on a journey of discovery themselves. If they wanted to find the truth about something, it was usually easier to look up what Aristotle or other ancient scholars had said about it. The classical writers had become authorities viewed with the more authoritarian values of Galilee and Rome.

The question for medieval scholars was how to interpret what the ancients said, rather than replicate their findings. Indeed, replication of many classical observations would have been impossible in England. The sky, plants, animals, politics, religion and social behaviour were different in Greece.

The lecture system developed because not everyone could look up what the ancients said for themselves. There were too few manuscripts and not everyone could read classical Latin and Greek. A lecture was something literally read from a "lectern".

Discussion was still the central process to resolve disagreements, but the technique of disputation was more commonly used. As in our parliament and our law courts, this tended to be a two-sided contest rather than one displaying a diversity of possible opinions. It had one interesting technique which would be good for students to use occasionally today: before replying to opponents, they were expected to summarise their arguments. This not only encouraged accurate listening and understanding, but it also produced more appreciation of the merits of the opponent's case.

We should not demean the medieval scholars, but their reliance upon the authority of the classics, the Church and the State runs contrary to our modern emphasis upon encouraging students to observe and think for themselves. There is a story that several monks were considering the question of how many teeth a horse has. They looked at all the documents and sources of reference they could lay their hands on and debated long and hard all day and well into the night. With this question still unresolved and when it was getting very late, one young monk ventured to ask if he might be allowed to speak. On permission being granted, he suggested that right now they should take a lantern, go down to the stables, open the mouth of the horse, count its teeth and settle the matter. Whereupon the elders turned upon him, and chastised his impudence for supposing that his own observations could outweigh the opinions of all the scholars that had ever preceded him.

This subservience should warn ordinary citizens in Britain today, that society will stagnate if the universities are allowed to be dominated by the wealthy, the Church or the State. When writing for the first edition of this book in June 1989, Chinese tanks were rolling into Tiannamen Square, Beijing, to suppress with brutality the peaceful democratic aspirations of students. The soldiers had been given false information. False confessions were shown on Chinese television. You see, truth was the first casualty. Truth is what universities exist to seek and proclaim. That is why university students have often been prominent throughout history when similar events have occurred.

In Britain it was not until the Renaissance, the Reformation and the scientific revolution that followed, that the mould of medieval thought began to be broken. Even then, it was not the universities that broke it. Nevertheless those changes are part of the heritage of higher education.

III.   The growing freedoms of expression, opinion, observation and criticism
The 15th, 16th and 17th centuries slowly established hard won liberties that constantly have to be defended.

First there was a new found freedom of expression in the arts, particularly in Italy (the Italian Renaissance) and Elizabethan England. But the resistance of the Church meant that the study of arts stayed mostly outside the universities. Painting, musical performance, sport, sculpture, dance and ballet, to name but a few, remained largely outside the higher education system until very recently. Yet without the free expression of imagination and feelings, there cannot be a genuine search for truths, values and ideas. Without that search, education will not be *higher* education. It is a freedom that tutors in arts and humanities today try to release in their students, often to undo the conformity of schools. When successful, parents find their values challenged.

Second there was a humanist movement. It was an intellectual movement, initially preaching tolerance, ridiculing the hypocrisy of the Church and reinterpreting the Athenian legacy with the aid of new documents and scholars arriving from Greece after the fall of Constantinople in 1453. Its importance for higher education today lies in a new confidence in humanity - that people can learn for themselves and exercise their own judgement. This confidence is something higher education today constantly strives to give its students. In short, Renaissance humanism gave a new value to individuals – their beliefs, their rights and their feelings. Without it, the Reformation - the breaking away of the Church of England and the Lutheran Church from the Church of Rome - would not have been possible. Equally, although men and women continued for some time to be persecuted for their beliefs, the break gave a political freedom that in turn reinforced the greater value for the individual.

Individualism permits original thinking. Originality is the first step to human advancement and is the essence of research. That is why human advancement and higher education go together. The greater value and confidence in individuals naturally lead to more trust in their powers of observation as a way of gaining knowledge. That is fundamental to modern science.

Third, the dormant seeds of scientific thought sown in Athens 1,800 years before, were germinated. To quote Bertrand Russell's *History of Western Philosophy*,

'It is not what the man of science believes that distinguishes him, but how and why he believes it. His beliefs are tentative, not dogmatic. They are based upon evidence, not upon intuition or authority. The founders of modern science showed great patience in observation and great boldness in forming their hypotheses. The authority of science is intellectual, not governmental. No penalties befall those who reject it; acceptance is not motivated by prudence. It prevails by its intrinsic appeal to reason. It is moreover, a piecemeal and partial authority. It does not, like Catholic dogma, lay down a complete system covering human morality, the past and future history of the universe.'

The tentativeness of academic integrity produces a temper of mind very different from the dogmas of autocrats or the Church.

These three things are concerned with the right to express one's opinions and feelings openly, the value of individual human beings and the pursuit of truth. No doubt they are not absolutes, but they are values fundamental to higher education. They are values that were contrary to those of the Church at that time and that fact has had a profound effect upon curricula in schools and colleges ever since. The values of the Church were based upon discipline not free expression, faith not doubt, corporate wisdom not individualism, and bookish learning not scientific observation.

IV.   The struggle to establish science, technology and practical subjects

Throughout the 16th, 17th and 18th centuries the most important intellectual and cultural advances were made outside higher education. True, Sir Thomas More the political theorist, Harvey the physician, Hobbes and Locke the philosophers, and Sir Isaac Newton the astronomer and mathematician all went to a university; and that may have strengthened the mythical belief that a classical education fits you for anything. But they did not do their significant work there. Others, not least Shakespeare and Sir Francis Bacon, never went to university at all. The same might be said about Michelangelo, Leonardo, Galileo, Pascal and others on the continent of Europe.

Science seemed to conflict with religion. In England the Church effectively controlled the schools and the universities by its system of endowments and it did not encourage the study of science. The division of knowledge into arts and sciences is still with us. Admission to Oxford and Cambridge was not possible without religious tests until after 1854. Except in Scotland, little science or engineering, except mathematics and medicine, was taught until after the Devonshire Commission of 1872.

In England the greatest interest in science, inventions, discoveries and new ideas was in clubs and societies meeting in most of the major cities, not in the two universities of Oxford and Cambridge. For example, the Royal Society was founded in 1660, societies for literature and architecture in the 1730s, the British Museum in 1753, the Royal Society of Arts, Manufacturing and Commerce in 1754, the Royal Institution in 1799 and the British Association for the Advancement of Science in 1831.

Notice that although the two universities in England were mostly attended by young gentlemen who might spend a life of leisure, science too, was a leisure pursuit for the wealthy. Working men who wanted to study science in an applied way went to the Mechanics Institutes and Working Men's Clubs which were opening in the evenings in many cities.

The concept of a university was that it taught bookish subjects. Arts such as painting, architecture, music, agriculture, navigation, dance, acting, government, engineering and many others were not only not taught, their practitioners were too often regarded as inferior people. Practical and manual skills were given low status. It was, and sometimes still is, assumed that the bright children at school will go on to further study, while the less intelligent will do practical work.

These prejudices are still with us. They are socially divisive, educationally narrow and conceptually mistaken. Professions and organisations wanting to improve their educational standards, set up their own colleges outside the universities. That is why specialist professional colleges in agriculture, music, art, technology and paramedical subjects, were at first established outside the education system. By the 1850s there were over 50 teacher training colleges, almost all supported by religious foundations.

So the fragmentation of higher education provision has deep historical roots based upon bookish learning and attitudes about what is academically respectable. Only in the last 20 years has reintegration within a higher education system made significant progress. Even now, vested and political interests, assumptions about subject boundaries, prejudices about combining practical and theoretical skills, preconceptions about other people's occupations and professions, and traditions of organisation and finance too often get in the way.

It was only with the coming of the Industrial Revolution that the joint pressure of scientists, the London medical schools, Catholics, nonconformists, liberals, free thinkers and others successfully demanded a university that would teach beyond the Oxbridge curriculum. University College, London, was founded by Jeremy Bentham in 1827 on condition that no religion was taught in it. He believed education should be directly useful. Like the four Scottish universities it taught law, economics, medicine, mathematics, chemistry, modern languages and moral philosophy as well as the classics. It was non-residential. Its exams were taken by working and middle class men studying at home and at colleges such as the Mechanics Institutes and Working Men's Colleges. By 1849 it also admitted women, although women were not awarded degrees until 1878.

Thus a second tradition of British higher education became established. On the one hand, Oxbridge was aristocratic, clerical, elitist, concentrating on a liberal education in arts and humanities, and providing mainly non-vocational courses. Its staff and students were well connected with people in national positions of power and providing 70% of the civil service. On the other hand, in the second half of the 19th century several of the industrial cities, such as Manchester, Birmingham, Leeds and Sheffield, established civic universities which were locally supported, vocationally oriented, closely related to, and dependent upon, local business and industry with middle-class students largely living at home.

These two traditions represent a conflict between the ideals of a general liberal education and a vocational education that is still with us. Today many people will see older universities as representing the traditional liberal values, while the former polytechnics and colleges in the public sector have vocational ideals. But that is a mistake. The conflict is in our minds, not between institutions. All institutions embody both ideals.

You may think I have made the same mistake. I have portrayed the growth of science, technology and vocational education as if it was a process of overcoming the clerical and aristocratic resistance of other worldly academics in ivory towers at Oxbridge. There was some truth in that before the 19th century; but that resistance was even stronger in the worlds of commerce, business and industry. Well into the 1950s many employers hesitated to take on science and engineering graduates.

That conflict reached its peak in the middle of the 19th century. It is hard to realise now, that education was still seen by many people as the prerogative of the Church or other religious organisations, not the State or the individual. The greatest advocate of this viewpoint in higher education was Cardinal Newman whose opinions I dealt with in Chapter 2. Newman believed the first step in intellectual training is to learn to apply a system of rules. That is why a schoolboy's education (the education of girls does not seem to enter Newman's scheme of things) should begin with Grammar and then Mathematics. The Grammar is the grammar of Latin and Greek.

This view of learning had a strong influence on school curricula because headmasters saw universities as the path to success. The idea that "Grammar" schools were for the most intelligent who aspire to higher education, technical schools were for those with practical skills and senior schools were for unskilled workers, persisted until the 1944 Education Act and, arguably, for another 20 years beyond that. White collar workers have long been seen as superior to engineers or those who make things or do manual or physical work. As late as 1960, Advanced-Level Latin or Greek was a necessary entry qualification for undergraduates seeking arts degrees at London University. Only very recently have employment-based skills begun to find a place in educational curricula. "Education" has been conceived as academic, whilst "training" has been seen as more practical and vocationally relevant. Even to this day the fee-paying schools send more students to university to study arts subjects, while state comprehensive schools send more undergraduates to study science.

Science is an activity. It is a process of discovery. It is more concerned with experiment than studying books. It involves research more than scholarship. Thus it was that the growth of science in higher education also meant the growing recognition of research as a service offered by civic universities to local industry and governments. Notice, it was 'science', not 'applied science' or 'engineering'. Even to this day, engineering is often the poor relation of science. This linkage of science and research came from Germany which was a growing scientific and military power in the late 19th and early 20th centuries. It is small wonder that British governments took fright and said 'we must have scientific and military research too' and the universities increasingly said 'OK, but you must pay for it'. They both still do.

The makings of the modern system
V.   The age of Government support and the "buffer principle"
There has been a growing demand for student places throughout the 19th and 20th centuries. Higher education has been seen as the path to success. In addition, as I've just said, from the 1850s professors were increasingly expected to do research. These two factors placed strain upon university resources. From 1889 onwards the Government helped universities financially from time to time. At the end of the First World War there were a large number of returning heroes who wanted to go to university.

Accordingly, in 1919 the Treasury authorised a University Grants Committee (UGC) "To enquire into the financial needs of university education in Great Britain; and to advise the Government as to the application of any grants that may be made by Parliament towards meeting them." The Committee, established almost casually, continued for 70 formative years until it was replaced by the Universities Funding Council in 1989. (See IX The age of excellence.)

By its formation the Government tacitly recognised that the provision of higher education is a matter of national concern, not merely a private matter. And it recognised its responsibility to maintain it. Even more important, a "buffer" was created between the Government and the universities - the Buffer Principle. That is, the Government of the day acknowledged the freedom of the universities to manage their own affairs without interference, even though they were partly funded by

Government. That was less an academic freedom for individuals; more a managerial freedom for institutions.

Many people, particularly those from abroad, find the buffer principle difficult to understand. Perhaps an analogy is the best way to explain this freedom. The Government pays the salary of the Leader of the Opposition in Parliament because it is recognised that good government requires an effective and respected opposition. The opposition should expose incompetence by effectively publicising its view of the truth. It is also the job of higher education to seek and publicise alternative views of the truth. That includes truths that may either support or oppose the Government view. The assumption that higher education exists purely for the sake of those engaged in it, (who should therefore bear its total cost) is wholly misleading. It has an important role in the preservation of democracy and good government that is worth paying for. That is why the Government has a responsibility to pay for it.

The reason is constitutional. It is the disinterested objectivity of university researchers that should be crucial to their critique of government. This is clouded when governments penalise them for their opinions or where a quasi monopoly of information is held by governments.

At first the proportion of university income from government grants was small. Over the years it has increased not only because the number of students has increased, new buildings have been required and new universities have been established, but because the nation has required a great deal of research. Government funding of both teaching and research is known as "the dual support system" or "dual funding".

In financing university research, governments have also recognised that they have a special responsibility to fund universities for financial and strategic reasons. Much of the research has been fundamental, such as research into the nature of the atom. This research was not of immediate use to industry, but was invaluable later (e.g. for the nuclear power industry). Naturally it is part of the nature of research that you don't always know what you are going to find out. If you did, there would often be no point in doing it. By financing fundamental research, the Government recognised that it has a responsibility to risk funding research with uncertain or long delayed benefits and high set-up costs. No one in the commercial world could reasonably take such long term and costly risks.

VI.   The age of expansion

During the years immediately after the Second World War, government had two priorities for higher education:- to double the number of science students within five years; and to provide emergency training for teachers, especially mature students leaving the armed forces after conscription. The first, achieved early, was because of the importance of science and technology in winning the war; the second was to compensate for losses during the war and also to prepare for the raising of the school leaving age.

After this burst, the numbers of students fell slightly during the 1950s. The emphasis on science and technology continued with the development of regional technical colleges, later called Colleges of Advanced Technology, under the control of

Local Education Authorities. During the 1950s the provincial "redbrick" universities in England were given full charters, independent academically of the University of London. There was steady growth in numbers of students later in the decade.

1963 was a crucial date in the development of British higher education. In that year the Robbins Report on Higher Education was published. The Robbins Committee said that "courses of higher education should be available for all those who are qualified by ability and attainment to pursue them and who wish to do so". This is often known as the "Robbins Principle" and has formed one basis of higher education thinking ever since. The principle was justified, firstly on the grounds that a nation's economic growth and higher cultural standards can only be achieved by making the most of the talents of its citizens; and secondly, because "the good society desires equality of opportunity for its citizens to become not merely good producers but also good men and women".

The Robbins principle confirmed the big expansion of higher education which had already been planned. In 1963 the birth rate appeared to be rising steeply (see Figure 3.1). The Committee believed that demand for full time higher education would rise from 216,000 places in 1962-63 to 390,000 in 1973-74 and 560,000 in 1980-81. The Committee, however, added a proviso that is often forgotten: that, for educational and vocational reasons, broader courses for the first degree should be taken by a much greater number of students. The Committee wanted less early specialisation and more students taking more than one main subject.

Universities were to provide 350,000 of the 560,000 full-time places needed in 1980-81. Six new universities were established; nine Colleges of Advanced Technology

Figure 3.1   Live births in England and Wales.

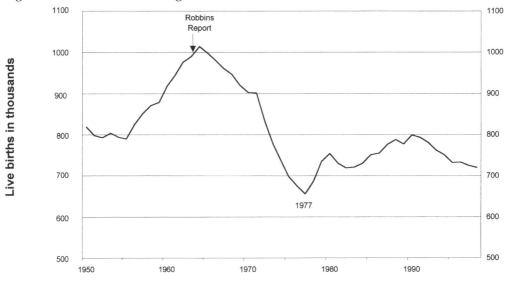

(CATs) and two Central Institutions (CIs) in Scotland were given university status; and many existing universities were expected to expand to 8,000 or 10,000 places. The Committee envisaged a hierarchy of regional, area and local colleges without university status. These colleges were encouraged to develop a wider range of advanced full time-courses to be validated in future by a Council for National Academic Awards (CNAA) which would cover the whole of Great Britain, would be established under a Royal Charter and should establish degree standards equivalent to those of the universities.

The Committee also recommended that there should be an increase in the number and status of teachers with the opportunity for professional training to be extended from three to four years to enable teachers to obtain the degree of Bachelor of Education (B.Ed.). It was intended that there should be 145,000 places for intending teachers in colleges of education.

Although both the major political parties accepted the Robbins Report at the time, its recommendations posed a problem for future governments since they implied increasing expenditure by both central and local government. New universities, new buildings, more staff and more facilities involved increasing capital and recurrent expenditure by central Government. New and expanding regional, area and local colleges involved new expenditure by local government. Moreover acceptance by the government of the Anderson Report in 1962 had led to a commitment to supply apparently ever growing numbers of students with grants. These difficulties were to come to a head in the late 1970s and early 1980s.

VII.   The age of equality

As well as confirming the period of expansion, the Anderson Report with its grants for all eligible students and the Robbins Report with its famous "principle" ushered in a period of movement towards equality in higher education. All those eligible and wishing to partake of higher education were not only to be found places, but were to be provided with the financial means necessary for their studies.

Recognising the need for more higher education places and particularly the needs of vocationally orientated students, Anthony Crosland, the Minister of Education, announced, in 1965 in a speech at Woolwich, that 30 new institutions called polytechnics would be established by upgrading and merging existing institutions. Polytechnic courses were to be academically validated by the CNAA, not by universities. They would be financed by local government contributing to a central pool from which central Government would allocate the funds. Compared with universities, polytechnics were to provide more occupationally related courses, to be more concerned with teaching than research and to be more locally based. This implied more home based students, more ties with industry and commerce, and a greater variety of full-time, part-time, sandwich, 'evenings only' and short term courses. The balance between arts and science courses should be strongly weighted to science and technology.

Crosland thereby gave voice to the "binary system" in which there were 'independent' universities on the one hand and a range of institutions under some form of greater governmental control on the other. Under the binary policy, an institution was on one side or the other of a binary line dividing the 'private' and 'public' sectors. This situation was to be a feature of higher education until the Further and Higher Education Act of 1992.

The Robbins Committee had believed that universities would respond to the challenge of producing more innovative and occupationally related courses. In the event, while some universities attempted innovations, most expansion was 'more of the same'. There was a swing away from science and vocationally orientated courses amongst applicants from schools. Universities were loath to turn away students in the arts and humanities by offering science and engineering places that could not be filled.

Meanwhile the polytechnics expanded, matured and developed their own individuality. The reputation of the CNAA grew. Many local authorities viewed their polytechnics with justifiable pride, as they had the civic universities 80 years earlier, and encouraged the diversity of courses for which they were established. By the end of the 1970s, however, it was clear that the polytechnics too had expanded far more in arts and humanities than in science and technology. It had been cheaper to do so and they had responded to student demand.

Equality was also on the minds of students in the 1960s. In 1968, there were world-wide student protests seeking more representation in university and college affairs, and more occupational relevance in their courses. It is the students who lived through that period who are now the parents of the current generation of students who in many respects have become conditioned by the right wing Thatcher Government to many of the principles against which their parents protested. One of the legacies of the period was increased student representation on decision-making bodies within institutions. Over time this has strengthened the voice of students in their rise towards the status of clients of their institution and even partners in the learning enterprise, reinforced by an increase in the number of postgraduate and mature undergraduate students.

And what equality of opportunities should be provided for potential students who had missed out on higher education at the standard age of 18 plus? In 1969, a new form of university was established to meet the needs of part-time, home-based students. The Open University uncovered an unsuspected demand for continuing education and has provided a valuable service for hundreds of thousands of students who would not otherwise have had the opportunity for a university education. It teaches by high quality learning texts supported by local tutors and in some cases residential schools and audio/visual material.

The growing cost of higher education was not going unnoticed, however. In 1969, Shirley Williams, the then Minister for Higher Education, asked universities to consider a number of reforms that would reduce such costs. Known as the "thirteen points", these reforms would have included the reduction of student grants, substituting loans, requiring students to undertake specified employment for a period after graduation, and requiring more students to be resident at home. The style was consultative. The Vice Chancellors were not very receptive. Had they been, the traumatic events of the early 1980s might have been avoided. Most of the "thirteen points" are now established policy.

VIII.   The age of efficiency

From the early 1970s until the present day the funding to produce a graduate has virtually halved in real terms (see Figure 3.2). It's been a period of increasing efficiency. But it didn't seem so. Because inflation was high and student numbers were rising steeply, costs were rising. So the money spent seemed like a sharp increase. In 1975, under inflationary pressure caused by the oil crisis of the period, the Government abandoned the quinquennial system in which funding for universities was based on a five year programme. Unlike the polytechnics which under local authority control only ever had one year budgets, the quinquennial system had given to universities a degree of certainty in their future planning. No such certainty was to return.

In the middle of the decade many teacher training colleges were closed or merged with polytechnics. A few merged with universities; a few more diversified into colleges of higher education. The reason was a dramatic fall in the birth rate after 1964 resulting from the easier availability of condoms, the pill and abortion. (See Figure 3.1.) Following from Mrs Thatcher's 1972 White Paper called, without irony, "A Framework for Expansion", the 143,000 students in teacher training were reduced by about 100,000. The universities being more prestigious, the 'public' sector bore the brunt of most of this turmoil. Its numbers reduced whilst the traditional universities continued to expand slowly. In 1978, as a further cost cutting measure, the Government insisted that students from overseas should not be subsidised by the British taxpayer and as a consequence universities were forced to charge higher fees to overseas students. In 1981 further increases led to the charging of "full cost" fees. Students from the European community, however, avoided such increases on the basis of reciprocal arrangements. There was great concern that damage would be done to Commonwealth

Figure 3.2   Index of public funding per student for higher education 1976-7 to 1997-8.
Source: Department for Education and Employment

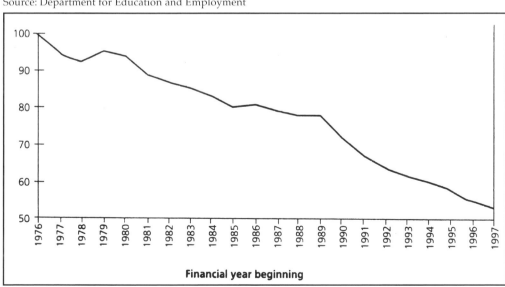

and international relations, but after an initial period of uncertainty the attraction of a university education in Britain was recognised and today many universities have a substantial number of overseas students. Now, their fees are going down as British, Asian and Australasian universities compete to attract them. These students reinforce the international dimension of higher education and bring significant income to the institutions they attend.

In 1979 a Conservative Government was returned to power. At that stage it probably did not have a clear strategy for higher education but it did have a clear policy of reducing public expenditure and destroying local government's roles. It was inevitable that universities and polytechnics would suffer financially. Previous governments had used many academics as advisers. The Thatcher Government used more industrialists and financiers. Naturally their values were overwhelmingly financial. A simplistic impression was given that industrialists produced wealth while education and social services consumed it; and that education was not producing graduates with the right employable skills. All of this was denied by the evidence to the Parliamentary Select Committee chaired by Christopher Price which reported in 1981. To the Government, however, education was seen as a cost rather than an investment. It is an irony that internationally it was British higher education which had such a high reputation for research and inventiveness and yet was being made a scapegoat for the poor performance of the British economy.

With the expected fall in the number of 18 to 20 year-olds from 1983 onwards,

Figure 3.3   Higher education Age Participation Index.
Source: Department for Education and Employment

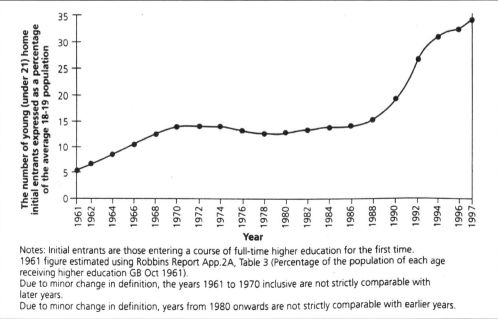

Notes: Initial entrants are those entering a course of full-time higher education for the first time.
1961 figure estimated using Robbins Report App.2A, Table 3 (Percentage of the population of each age receiving higher education GB Oct 1961).
Due to minor change in definition, the years 1961 to 1970 inclusive are not strictly comparable with later years.
Due to minor change in definition, years from 1980 onwards are not strictly comparable with earlier years.

higher education was an obvious target for reduced public expenditure whilst maintaining the proportion of the 18-21 age group who entered. (See Figure 3.3.) Funding to the universities and the public sector institutions was cut by nearly 20%. Furthermore, tuition fees were halved, not to help those students who paid their own fees, but to remove the incentive for institutions to replace their income by recruiting more students whose fees would be paid by central government via local education authorities. In succeeding years fees went up and down depending upon government policy towards expansion or consolidation.

The size and impact of these cuts differed between universities and represented a potential retreat from the "Robbins Principle ". In order to protect, at least to some extent, the amount of money available per student, the UGC restricted student entry, but growth in public sector institutions enabled the government to claim that in practice there continued to be a place somewhere in higher education for all those qualified and seeking to enter.

Some, vocal, industrialists believed higher education was poorly managed and if only higher education were organised like industry, it would be less expensive and more efficient. Spurred by criticisms and the threat of a Government enquiry, in 1984 The Committee of Vice-Chancellors and Principals (CVCP) set up their own Committee under the chairmanship of Sir Alex Jarratt, a prominent industrialist, to study the 'efficiency' of universities. The Committee was solely concerned with the management of universities, not its academic or educational policies, practices and methods.

The Jarratt Committee made some useful recommendations to Government, the University Grants Committee (UGC), the CVCP itself and to universities in general. It proposed that the Government should facilitate long term planning in universities by suggesting broad policy guidelines and restoring a longer term funding horizon as there used to be with the quinquennial system. It recommended a review of the role of the UGC and wanted to encourage it to collaborate more closely with universities by making its views known and increasing discussion of them. It suggested that a range of performance indicators should be developed to enable comparisons between universities and that the CVCP should extend its training of senior university personnel. It advised universities to have rolling academic and institutional plans, more budget delegation in a hierarchy of cost centres, and more staff development, appraisal and accountability in the light of these plans and delegated financial responsibilities. It also advocated stronger "management", separate from academic leadership. These recommendations have had a considerable effect. The devolution of financial responsibility to cost centres roughly corresponding to academic departments, created much more financial awareness and economy amongst staff below head of department level. For 20 years, staff development activities had been ignored, if not resisted, by many academic staff. With the introduction of appraisal schemes, initially strongly urged by government during salary negotiations, and more confident support by Vice-Chancellors, these activities became more widely recognised and acceptable. In 1982 the Government had set up a National Advisory Body for Local Authority Higher Education (NAB) to allocate the money according to what courses should be encouraged in the national interest in public sector institutions. This represented half a step away from LEA control. In 1985, the Government asked the NAB to carry out a review of public sector management similar to that undertaken by the Jarratt Committee for universities. Many of the recommendations in terms of financial management and increased public accountability were similar. Most were implicit in the Education Reform Act of 1988.

IX.   The age of excellence

Just as the late 1970s and early 1980s had been a period during which efficiency had seemed to dominate the government's thinking on higher education, so in the late 1980s and into the 1990s the government placed its emphasis on concepts of quality and excellence. This should not be surprising. With a move from an elite to a mass system of higher education it is natural that questions should be asked about the quality of teaching and research being provided within the wider range of institutions offering higher education. It is also natural that the public should expect institutions to be accountable for the way in which they use public funds.

Consistent with the Government's policy of a more direct involvement with the future direction of higher education, the Education Reform Act of 1988 replaced the University Grants Committee and the National Advisory Board with the Universities Funding Council (UFC) and the Polytechnics and Colleges Funding Council (PCFC). Both the UFC and the PCFC had 15 members appointed by the Secretary of State, of whom 6 to 9 had experience and competence in the field of higher education; whilst the remainder had experience in the fields of industry, commerce and finance. The Act also turned polytechnics and colleges of higher education into free standing statutory corporations, thus representing the final break from LEA control. For the first time they could now, for instance, invest and accumulate reserves in the same way as universities had always been allowed to do. By the mid 1980s it had been felt that the polytechnics had come of age and should be capable of awarding their own degrees rather than being subject to the CNAA. This process is directly analogous to the way many newer civic universities became independent in the 1950s, having previously offered degrees of the University of London, as mentioned above. From 1988 onwards, polytechnics and other colleges could apply for independence to validate their own degrees for a period of five years. 20 years earlier, polytechnics and colleges of education were seen as locally based teaching institutions. Now they were recognised as national, if not international, institutions.

The Education Reform Act of 1988, did not, however, mark the end of the transformation of higher education. Four years later the Further and Higher Education Act, 1992, saw the abandonment of the binary line. Polytechnics were granted university status, the UFC and the PCFC were replaced by the Higher Education Funding Council for England (HEFCE) and similar bodies for Scotland and Wales. The Act also placed a duty on the funding councils to develop wide-ranging systems of quality assessment.

Concerned at the possibility of external bodies assessing the quality of higher education, institutions themselves established the Higher Education Quality Council (HEQC) to conduct audits to ensure that quality assurance procedures were in place and operational within each institution. There thus developed a dual system:- the HEQC conducted institutional audits whilst the Funding Councils conducted subject reviews of teaching and continued the practice of research assessment exercises (RAE) begun by the UGC in 1986. The teaching quality assessments (TQA) commenced by using a grading scale of excellent, satisfactory or unsatisfactory. (See Chapter 11.) This system was subsequently expanded to the grading of six core aspects of provision according to a four-point scale. Published reports followed each assessment. At the time of writing a new Quality Assurance Agency has been established to provide a consolidated approach to quality issues. These teaching assessments did not directly affect funding (except in Scotland), but the RAE was a direct attempt by Government to introduce selectivity in the funding of research. (See Chapter 11.) Exercises were conducted in 1986, 1989, 1992, and 1996. The assessment scale varied between years but by 1996 a seven-point scale was being employed. The funding councils allocated funds according to the grade achieved and the number of "research active" staff that had been submitted for assessment. More details of the funding methodology will be given in Chapter12.

Both TQA and RAE involved a considerable amount of work on the part of institutions, Funding Councils and HEQC. They also affected the way in which institutions and individuals reacted. Institutional quality assurance mechanisms were strengthened as a result and although the impetus had initially been on accountability, over time the emphasis changed to one of staff development and mechanisms for self-improvement. Research activity meanwhile was becoming more managed with a team approach. The concept of the loan researcher particularly in the sciences could no longer be afforded. Whilst the concept of the RAE was to increase selectivity in the allocation of research funds it also had the effect of stimulating departments without a history of research to focus on such activities as a means of increasing income. The Funding Councils responded by raising the threshold for the receipt of research funds but with an overall improvement of grades departments had constantly to improve their grading to stand still in cash terms.

In terms of student numbers, the reduction in unit cost per student imposed by the Government (Figure 3.2), required 'efficiency savings'. Many institutions managed this by expansion. They generated more income *in total* by increasing student numbers. From 1993, Government stopped expansion - the funding councils 'fined' institutions that recruited more than an agreed number of students. This was because students still attracted fee payments and some reduced grant from LEAs, even if institutions received no more money directly from the funding council. Eventually, some vice-chancellors threatened to introduce "top-up fees" to compensate for reductions in government funding; the organisation of loans was inefficient and just as expensive in the short-term as grants. The backlog of buildings maintenance was creating health and safety concerns. Research in science and medicine was increasingly expensive. In 1996, this threatened to become a major issue in the impending election and both major parties agreed to a Committee of Inquiry into Higher Education under Sir Ron Dearing to take the issue off the immediate agenda. This Committee of Inquiry was hailed as a 'new Robbins', but the report was disappointing. It lacked vision; dealt with small details; and had its major recommendation on funding rejected by Government on the day it appeared. The dominance of economic policy over higher education can be seen in the delay by Government in responding to most recommendations requiring resources until the Comprehensive Spending Review of Government overall in 1998.

Summary

In this chapter we have tried to summarise 2,500 years of higher education. In recent years higher education has been dominated by ideas of opportunity, equality, efficiency and quality. These managerial and financial issues include the rise in student numbers and age participation rates in the 1960s and the 1990s shown in Figures 3.3 and the decline in public funding per student shown in Figure 3.2.

Yet if you keep the years in perspective, no matter how you balance the aims of higher education considered in Chapter 2, the underlying values are rightly academic and intellectual, not managerial and financial. They are the pursuit and proclamation of the truth as one sees it.

While people through the ages have had ideas of the truth fitting their time and culture, there are also fundamental ideas about the nature of knowledge and how it is obtained which have burned like lanterns, sometimes brightly, sometimes dimly when blown by the winds of oppression. If ever they are blown out, our civilisation will suffer a loss of freedom and a loss of progress. To seek the truth is fundamental to freedom. To apply it is fundamental progress.

Further reading

Pratt, J. (1997) The Polytechnic experiment, Open University Press, Buckingham
Shattock, M. (ed) (1996) The Creation of a University System, Oxford, Blackwell.

4. Understanding the New Higher Education System

The Further and Higher Education Acts of 1992 changed the face of higher education in Britain. No longer is there a binary line between the universities and the polytechnics. Now they are all part of four unitary systems funded by the Higher Education Funding Councils for England, Scotland and Wales and the Department of Education in Northern Ireland.

This "seamless robe", however, disguises many differences between institutions. Indeed now that there are so many institutions with the title of university, it has become even more important for them to establish their own mission and identity. Moreover a significant amount of higher education provision (12% in England; 20% in Scotland) is found, not in universities, but in further education institutions. This has found expression in more overt marketing policies, but can still be confusing to anyone looking at British higher education for the first time. This chapter aims to clarify the picture.

Unlike the situation in many other European countries, universities are not directly responsible to the Government and their staff are not civil servants. In this sense they are private institutions although receiving a high proportion of their funds from Government. Universities are concerned to gain new knowledge and insights by research and scholarship as well as to teach. Community service is also emerging as a key function for many institutions. The balance between these activities is a matter for each institution but it has always been maintained that good teaching can only emanate from research and original scholarship. Some universities, however, are more research orientated than others and recent funding pressures have often forced universities to be selective about their research efforts. It is remarkable, however, how many students arrive at university unaware of this dual function.

Universities design, validate and administer their own courses, student assessments and awards. The vast majority of full-time students take courses leading to bachelor's, master's or doctoral degrees. There are several different kinds of university resulting from their past history.

I. Oxbridge

Oxford and Cambridge are ancient universities founded in the Middle Ages each with many different colleges forming the university. Financially the colleges are well endowed. The centres of both cities are dominated by the universities. College residences and a chapel are often round a courtyard, the entrance to which is past a porter's lodge and a scattered array of bicycles.

Students apply for entry to a residential college not to the university, but there are also separate academic departments. Applicants with breadth, depth and the ability to argue their own point of view are most likely to be selected. These colleges offer scholarships and exhibitions (minor scholarships) to the best applicants, the value of which lies more in their prestige than their monetary value.

Unlike other universities the basic method of teaching is the tutorial. Each student is assigned to a tutor for whom, typically, that student writes a weekly essay, which is then critically discussed. Lectures have a supporting role and attendance is optional. This method develops individuality and independence of mind, articulate and balanced argument, the ability to research sources, and the capacity to work under pressure and to meet deadlines. It is expensive of staff time, but arguably worth it.

For many purposes St. Andrews, on the east coast of Scotland, should be included with Oxbridge. It is not so large, nor does it have many different colleges; but it is the oldest university in Scotland, predating the Reformation. Like Oxbridge, the university dominates the town. Indeed the town would scarcely exist if it were not for the university. It does not operate the same system of tutorial teaching; but it does offer some scholarships and it continues to attract good students, most of whom are English.

II.   Other Collegiate universities

In some of its organisational features the University of Durham, the third oldest university in England although lagging some years behind Glasgow, Aberdeen and Edinburgh, is also collegiate as are Lancaster and York. Usually described as federal institutions are the University of Wales with seven colleges, and London University, which is so enormous and scattered that its staff and students identify more with their college than their university. Many of the colleges have distinctive characters and their own international reputations for satisfying particular needs. For example, Imperial College has a formidable reputation for research in science and technology. The London School of Economics (LSE) is equally respected amongst social scientists. Birkbeck has a unique place in the provision of part-time evening degrees.

As many as 12 London medical schools have now merged to form six; some, like Guys and St. Thomas's, are better known to the general public than the University itself, so that ordinary people think of them only as hospitals, not as being part of a university. London University also includes numerous specialist institutions such as the Institute of Education, the School of Oriental and African Studies, the Institute of Psychiatry, the School of Hygiene and Tropical Medicine and the Royal Veterinary College. All have made internationally recognised contributions in their fields.

III.   Older Civic universities

The older civic universities are those that sprang up at the end of the nineteenth century in the rapidly growing industrial cities. Some of them grew from the adult education and trades union movements of that time, when, it must be remembered, secondary education was not generally available. Edinburgh, Aberdeen and Glasgow can also be included under this heading, though they are much older and have different origins. Although older civic universities now see themselves as international institutions, they retain some of their local interests (e.g. textiles at Leeds, music at Manchester, metallurgy at Sheffield). In particular they mostly have large "Extra-

Mural" departments originally serving their local communities with cultural non-vocational evening and daytime classes. In the 1980s these departments were strongly encouraged to provide vocational courses for credit in what is now called "Continuing Education". After Oxbridge, older civic universities demand the highest entry standards, as measured by A Level scores. They are able to teach a very wide range of subjects because, by the post-Robbins expansion in the 1960s, they were already mature institutions with a broad academic base on which to build specialist departments in what were then new fields (e.g. subjects within the broad fields of biotechnology and the information sciences). Furthermore, when the cuts came, units that were cut to a non-viable size were able to find other departments with which they could sensibly merge, rather than close altogether. By now, however, many are cramped for space and much of their older accommodation is inappropriate and expensive to maintain and heat.

IV.   Newer Civic universities

The newer civic universities (e.g. Exeter, Hull, Leicester, Nottingham, Reading and Southampton) were those whose students had taken London external degrees until the early 1950s. That was like a period of apprenticeship in which comparisons could be made between the standards of the various "university colleges", as they were called, against the standards of London. During the 1950s they obtained charters and were able to award their own degrees. Newcastle had a similar apprenticeship with Durham and could best be placed in this group.

Some of them have developed specialist reputations. Some of these are associated with local industries, for example mechanical, production, electrical, electronic and aeronautical engineering at Southampton all contribute to the aircraft industry. Pharmacy at Nottingham has long been supported by Boots, the chemists.

Some of the newer civic universities, for example Newcastle and Leicester, are like the older civics in that they occupy sites well within the built-up area of the city and they have built on all the available space. Some, such as Exeter and Hull, have green field sites, perhaps by taking a timely opportunity to move from humble beginnings in the city centre. This may mean that they have been multi-campus universities during a formative period.

V.   Post–War universities

In the post-war period, particularly after the Robbins Report, two new kinds of university were established. There were "new" universities, such as East Anglia, Stirling and Sussex, which were usually on large greenacre sites outside medium-sized towns. Some of these universities were established with new ideals. Keele, for instance, tried to tackle the problem of early specialisation by requiring all undergraduates to take a general course in their first year, followed by two subjects over a further three years. However the scheme did not attract large numbers of students. Sussex meanwhile adopted an inter-disciplinary approach, whilst Warwick saw itself as a limited company with entrepreneurial drive. Many universities of the period developed particular specialisms. These developments were often the result of one individual who attracted a considerable amount of research money, sponsorship and students when the rest of the university had difficulty, or so transformed a subject by his/her own insights that good staff and students were attracted to form a strong nucleus. Sociology at Essex, biochemistry at Dundee, management studies at Stirling and social administration at York are examples.

The second kind of university established in the post-war period were the former Colleges of Advanced Technology (the ex-CATs) which were upgraded to university status following the report of the Robbins Committee in 1964. These, like Aston, Bradford, City (London), Salford, Heriot-Watt, Strathclyde and the University of Wales Institute of Science and Technology (UWIST) were often sited in the middle of industrial cities. Others, like Bath and Surrey, which had been Battersea College of Technology, moved to green field sites.

Naturally the ex-CATs retained their former staffs - staffs who typically had already had ten years' experience in industry before joining the college during the late 1950s. Consequently many of them were not young researchers full of zest. Some may have resented being expected to do research when that was not part of the job they originally accepted. Some saw themselves as professionals with practical experience to pass on to students, rather than academics breaking new ground. So the research image of some ex-CATs was slow to develop. Such attitudes were to reappear in some of the institutions granted university status in 1992.

There were also reasons why the ex-CATs did not expand rapidly. First there was the swing against science in the late 1960s and early 1970s. The ex-CATs had few arts and humanities departments; most were strong in management. Science applicants were more likely to be attracted to universities with established reputations. The city-centre sites and local college origins meant that they had few student residences. As a result students have often had to choose between expensive rents or daily journeys from the suburbs, to be paid from ever depreciating grants. These factors made them appear less popular amongst student applicants than other universities. For example, although they tended to recruit many more mature students with work experience and professional qualifications so that they had a richness of a different kind, on school based entry qualifications, they compared unfavourably with other universities.

VI.   Post 1992 universities

The Further and Higher Education Act of 1992 allowed former polytechnics and a handful of colleges of higher education (for example Derby and Luton) to apply for university designation. Since then, all former polytechnics have become universities. Dearing called these "1992 universities" and we use this term later in the book.

When polytechnics were first established in the early 1970s it was thought that they would be different from universities in that:
- they were financed by the local authority;
- their degree courses would be validated by the CNAA with a range of other professional qualifications also offered;
- their students would mostly be local with varied attendance patterns;
- they would mostly teach science, technology and applied vocational subjects;

- they would build and maintain close relationships with local employers; and
- their effort would be devoted to teaching rather than research.

Over time, however, they became financed by a national advisory body (the NAB). They gained more independence in the validation of their degrees. They recruited nationally as well as locally. The number of courses in the arts, humanities and business increased. And in some polytechnics staff established a growing reputation for their research work. In short, since they were established, the polytechnics gradually became more like universities. But they were under-valued internationally and there was a need to recognise their growing status.

Most former polytechnics (e.g. East London) inherited old or inappropriate buildings in decaying parts of inner cities, but most local authorities viewed their polytechnics with pride and went to some expense to build or improve their physical facilities. For example, most of Bristol Polytechnic moved to purpose built accommodation on a green field site outside the city near to motorway and inter-city rail communications. North London University, on the other hand continues to operate on five sites in buildings typical of the 1920s or earlier. Others had to make use of existing inner city sites so that new accommodation was built taller. Once built, the sites provided little opportunity for expansion. In the mid-1970s, however, there was pressure to close dozens of colleges of education. Many such colleges were merged with, or taken over by, large polytechnic institutions (for example Birmingham, Manchester, Kingston, Oxford and Leeds) which thereby acquired pleasant facilities in suburban if not rural surroundings.

Managerially, mergers provide both opportunities and problems. They provide opportunities for new, original and exciting courses when merged staffs have complementary expertise. When they have similar expertise mergers may create a critical mass capable of creating a distinctive reputation. In practice human factors often intervene. It is not easy to develop working relationships with new colleagues when campuses are miles apart. Nor is it usually possible for students to travel from one site to another, owing to constraints of time and money.

VII.   Other Institutions

For those not familiar with the higher education scene the above description must seem complicated enough, but the picture does not end here. There are, for instance, a number of institutions, such as University College Suffolk, which may be offering higher education opportunities as part of their portfolio and have ambitions to gain university status. These institutions may be affiliated to, or will have their degree programmes validated by, a neighbouring university. There are also many regional and local colleges supported by local education authorities (LEAs) which have a large number of students, but only a small proportion studying above A Level standard. Typically some time in the past there may have been an ambitious head of department and local demand for a particular degree course or Higher National Diploma and the college may have sought validation from the CNAA or submitted its students for London external degrees. As to the future, the Government has supported a recommendation from the Dearing Committee that there should be growth here at the HND level. These LEA colleges also support large numbers of professional courses, for example in social work or business, which are above A Level in standard, but which are not framed in the academic mould.

There is also a range of institutions outside the government funded sector. The private University of Buckingham, for instance, received its royal charter in 1986 and relies on student fees for its degree programmes. Other specialist private colleges not covered by the Further and Higher Education Act include, for example, management colleges which charge fees for providing courses to the managers of industry, commerce and the professions; ecclesiastical colleges, largely for training ministers of religion, which are often supplemented by trusts and other endowments; and the College of Law which is supported by the legal profession. There are also a number of colleges, such as Richmond College, which are satellite colleges of American universities. Students may come for a semester (half a year), continuing their degree courses, but also gaining experience of a culture other than their own.

Further Reading

Department for Education and Employment, (1998) Higher Education for the 21st Century: Response to the Dearing Report. HMSO

5. Is it Worth Entering Higher Education?

Introduction

Probably. It depends what you want to do with your life; how far higher education is essential to that; and whether you succeed in your studies, get the qualification and reach your goal. If, as a career, you want to be a doctor, teacher, lawyer, engineer, vet, town planner, etc., a degree is an essential prerequisite. If you want to be a manager in commerce, it is not. In many other countries of the EU over 90 per cent of top managers have degrees, usually in law, economics or engineering; in the UK the figure is about 50 per cent. Many leading industrial figures have not had a university education, for example Sir John Harvey-Jones. In the media, many people are graduates, but, in the satire boom of the 1960s and 1970s, Willy Rushton was not; nor is Paul Merton, an icon of the 1990s. In politics, six members of John Major's cabinet were together at Cambridge, but he did not go to university. Nor, among post-war prime ministers, did Winston Churchill or Jim Callaghan. Were they any worse, or better, than Heath, Thatcher or Wilson?

Higher education can transform lives. Richard Hoggart's *"The uses of literacy"* celebrates it and its role in taking him from the working-class back streets of a Leeds suburb to be one of the leading figures in our intellectual culture. Many Open University graduates bubble with enthusiasm about the mind-changing, eye-opening experience it gave them (and not only at summer school!). Books such as Walter Ellis's *"The Oxbridge conspiracy"* and Jeremy Paxman's *"Friends in high places"* show the role of Oxbridge in allowing, or confirming, access to the powerful establishment. But there is a downside. Some Open University students record how they grew away from their partners. Young, full-time students can be very lonely. Up to 3% leave in their first term and another 1% do not return to campus after their first Christmas vacation back home. Others feel uprooted and may take years to re-root themselves in a new community.

This chapter is about the costs and benefits of study. Not only the economics, but the personal and social factors.

I.   What does it cost?

Table 5.1 is from a study quoted by the Dearing Committee. It shows that in 1995-96 the average expenditure by *full-time* students on courses for which mandatory grants were available was just over £5,000. The figures show a balance sheet of income and expenditure by socio-economic group, which allows some calculation of the effects of the changes in student support as from 1998. Note the different patterns of income across the groups.

The abolition of grants penalises poorer students over four times as much as the

	Socio-Economic Group					
	I	II	IIIn	IIIm	IV-V	Total
Average grant in £	382	820	1,414	1,548	1,716	1,191
Average assessed parental contribution	767	838	392	357	184	551
Average received parental contribution	2,061	1,277	591	480	233	874
Proportion with loan %	45%	50%	54%	57%	62%	54%
Average loan	591	618	670	710	763	663
Access/Hardship fund %	0%	5%	6%	6%	11%	6%
Total income from student support	**3,040**	**2,773**	**3,082**	**2,853**	**3,021**	**2,917**
% Employed in academic year	62%	67%	65%	70%	59%	66%
Average earnings per academic year	454	594	661	645	663	625
Average amount received as gift	660	571	416	335	196	449
Average borrowed on credit	156	270	313	257	256	272
Average benefits payments	3	42	173	105	126	97
Average sponsorship/charity	50	76	85	60	27	72
Average withdrawn from savings	435	327	270	254	174	290
Other income	248	170	203	87	36	153
Total income from other sources	**2,039**	**2,084**	**2,151**	**1,770**	**1,507**	**1,990**
Essential expenditure	2,623	2,845	3,331	3,035	3,384	3,058
Other expenditure	2,035	2,039	2,126	1,929	1,912	2,033
Total expenditure	**4,658**	**4,884**	**5,457**	**4,964**	**5,296**	**5,091**
Balance	**+421**	**-27**	**-224**	**-341**	**-768**	**-124**

Table 5.1   Student finance – income and expenditure by socio-economic group, 1996.
Compiled by Callender and Kempson 1996. Quoted by Dearing Report
Figures are in £ unless stated as percentages. Socio-economic groups: I Professional; II Intermediate; IIIn
Skilled Non-manual; IIIm Skilled Manual; IV Partly skilled; V Unskilled.

children of rich parents. The introduction of fees will re-balance that to some extent. It was thought that one third of students would pay no fees; one third, full fees (of £1,000); and one third, partial fees. All part-time students will pay full fees as they have always done. So, the average working-class student, for each year of study, will owe something like £2,500; the student from a professional class background, just over £1,700.

Finance is a major disincentive for part-time students, as many Open University surveys have shown. For such students, and others studying part-time, time is the major investment. Consequently there are social costs such as not spending quality time with one's family, a constrained social life, possible loss of earnings through reduced overtime and so on. For full-time students there is the additional cost of lost earnings whilst studying. The choice is learn before you earn; earn while you learn; or, for some mature students, earn before you learn.

Note that a significant amount of income in Table 5.1 assumes a parental contribution. For mature students it is usually spouse income that will be taken into account when means-testing students to decide the level of fee they will pay. The DfEE booklet suggests that no fees will be paid by students where the gross family income is about £23,000 a year (£450 a week) and such students will have access to a full loan. At the other end, a gross family income over £35,000 will mean payment of a full fee and a more limited loan facility under the government scheme. No government loans are available for fees, only for living costs. The level of loan available in any year is not announced much in advance, but it is likely to be close to the levels of grant plus loan previously available. For a year of study other than the final year that would mean, in 1998-99 price levels,

- £4370 for students in London,
- £3545 for those elsewhere, and
- £2805 for those at home.

For final year students, reduce the amounts by about 15 per cent.

All those are, of course, well below the 1996 costs that we looked at earlier. Students will need to earn even more, or borrow privately, to make up the deficit. There will be a hardship fund, but the amounts available are small. Universities and colleges have been urged to allow payment of fees by instalment. Some, recognising reality, have offices to help students find part-time, term-time work. Student unions also help in this way. Facilities such as libraries and computer centres extend opening into unsocial hours, even 24 hours a day, to recognise the need for access by students committed to working as well as studying.

Since all but a handful of students are adult, it is odd to make them dependent on a parental contribution. From 1999 the amount of government loan that can be borrowed is governed by family income. If parents, or spouses, refuse to contribute, the government is not helpful: 'There is no reason why parents should refuse to help their children in the future as they will be expected to contribute no more than they would have to under the current system'. The second part is strictly true, but the student will have to borrow more, so the moral pressure on parents and spouses will increase. The DfEE leaflet, available from LEAs, called *"Financial Support for Students"* gives full details of arrangements, including extra payments to a minority of students in particular circumstances.

Interest on loans is charged at the same level as inflation, so even if you don't need the loan, it is worth borrowing the money and investing it at a higher rate. In 1996, one in eight of students taking out a loan did this – they had no <u>need</u> of a loan for their expenses as a student. At the other end of the spectrum, that study showed a group of people opposed to debt on moral grounds, or afraid of their problems over repayment.

Repayments are related to earnings – government use the term 'income-contingent'

A	B	C	D
Annual income	Monthly repayments	Annual repayments	C as a % of A
Up to £10,000		nil	nil
£11,000	£7	£84	0.8%
£12,000	£15	£180	1.5%
£15,000	£37	£444	3.0%
£20,000	£75	£900	4.5%

Table 5.2   Repayment of loans related to income.

for this. The Student Loans Company will work with the Inland Revenue to collect the money through Pay As You Earn (PAYE) so that it is deducted from wages or salary like income tax or national insurance. The more you earn, the more you pay. The basic threshold is £10,000 a year gross (about £200 a week) and examples of repayments are presented in Table 5.2.

II.   What is the case for loans?

Those arguing for loans claim that
- income contingent loans are not a deterrent to students from poorer backgrounds
- students in higher education are now adults, unlike 1962 when mandatory grants were introduced. Adulthood implies self-reliance.
- when students are clients (payers) as well as consumers, they will pressure for quality improvement.
- the life-time gain from graduate status is more than the price being charged, and other costs of 'deferred gratification'.

Those against loans argue that
- higher earners pay more in tax so that graduates pay more tax, on average, anyway;
- graduates make fewer demands on other public and social services, so get less for their tax;
- the state *requires* graduate status for many occupations where central or local government or their agencies are the employers and students should not have to pay their future employers a 'training fee';
- students contribute to the process of knowledge production and development; they are, therefore, co-workers and should be paid.

In rejoining UNESCO after the election of New Labour, the Government associated the UK with Article 13 of the International Convention on Economic, Social and Cultural Rights which says that higher education "shall be made equally accessible to all, on the basis of capacity, by every available means, and in particular by *the progressive introduction of free education*". The emphasis is added to show that the UK is moving in the opposite direction.

The evidence from Australia and Eire, and early signs in the UK since the announcement, suggest that fees and grant abolition deter students, especially those where there has been no previous family involvement in higher education.

III.   What are the benefits?

On average, graduates are less likely to be unemployed than non-graduates; are likely to earn more when employed than non-graduates; and, on the basis of research in the USA, have longer life expectancy, fewer illnesses, more stable personal lives and more rational procreation patterns.

The main arguments in this domain, though, are economic. There is a need to distinguish between early career and life-long earnings. One study, for the DfEE by the Policy Studies Institute, focused on people born in 1970. At age 23-24 (i.e. by the mid 1990s) they found that:

• graduates had the same rate of unemployment as non graduates;

Table 5.3   Comparison of Post-University and Post-A Level earnings after 10 years.
Hogarth et al. 1997, citing Labour Force survey, quoted by Dearing Report

Characteristic of individual	Estimated hourly earnings
1. Male; 16 years of education; 10 years work experience; **first degree**; living in SE England; **professional** occupation; no disability; white	£14.12
2. as (1), but black	£12.91
3. as (1), but Indian sub-continent	£11.86
4. as (1), but female	£11.39
5. as (1), but disabled	£12.51
6. Male; 13 years of education; 10 years work experience; **A Levels**; living in SE England; **professional** occupation; no disability; white	£11.27
7. as (6), but black	£10.30
8. as (6), but Indian sub-continent	£9.46
9. as (6), but female	£9.08
10. as (6), but disabled	£9.98
11. Male; 13 years of education; 10 years work experience; **A Levels**; living in SE England; **clerical** occupation; no disability; white	£8.83
12. as (11), but black	£8.07
13. as (11), but Indian sub-continent	£7.41
14. as (11), but female	£7.12
15. as (11), but disabled	£7.82

- only 41% of graduates were in 'graduate' jobs; for those with a higher degree the figure was 56% (this confirms other research about graduates' assessment of the extent to which their jobs demand graduate skills);
- a degree improved the chances of a graduate/professional job by a factor of 1.85 for men and 3.22 for women compared with those with similar 'A Levels' who did not go on to higher education.
- non-graduate males earned 97% of their graduate counterparts' average salary; for women the figure is 95%. However, holders of NVQ4, usually gained by part-time study, earned more than graduates
- graduates in non-graduate jobs earned the same as their non-graduate counterparts
- projections of life-time differentials show that male non-graduates may expect to earn 86% of graduate earnings and women non-graduates 76%. But the gap is closing.
- non-graduates have a longer working life to age 60 than graduates – about 10% longer.

These figures suggest that the best bet is a job after school with sponsored part-time study to degree level. It is odd that some such schemes, offered by major companies, do not recruit to all the places on offer.

A second study, cited in the Dearing Report, compares different groups 10 years into their careers. The figures in Table 5.3 show continuing disadvantage in being black, or female or disabled, as well as of having lower qualifications.

If we look even later in life, a supplement to the Dearing Report suggests that 18 year old male entrants to full time higher-education, who then graduate, 'lose' over £40,000 while studying, but by their mid-forties will be earning £10,000 a year more than otherwise comparable non-graduates. It also cites research that suggests that the demand for graduates will exceed supply until 2016 AD.

Figures in this chapter have been *averages*. There will be variations depending on several factors, such as gender and race as shown in Table 5.3. Graduate employment varies by subject studied and place of study. Graduates from 'modern' universities are more likely to go into employment after graduation. Those from traditional universities are more likely to choose, or need, to pursue immediate postgraduate study. So paradoxically, more graduates from modern universities and colleges are employed, *and* unemployed, six months after graduation. Those with degrees in such as economics, law or medicine are likely in the long run to earn more than those graduating in philosophy or training to be social workers or teachers.

So, we are back where we started – it depends on the individual and what they want to do, how much they are willing to invest and their calculation of the risk, in making that investment, as to the chance of it paying off. What value will higher education add to each individual as a person and to the life they may lead? The calculation keeps changing:- many students decide they have studied the 'wrong' subject; many graduates do not work in the field of their qualification; the job market will fluctuate and the value placed on jobs may change. For example will the job market always indicate that investment bankers are so much more vital than teachers and others who earn only 20 per cent of their salary? More graduates applying could create a 'buyer's market' for employers who would lower salaries accordingly.

But the argument is not only about price; it is about value, and many of the gains are beyond price. These gains are the personal and social factors mentioned in the introduction to this chapter. They are hard to define precisely because they are personal. Suffice to say higher education gives an understanding of at least some aspects of the world. More important, it gives the capacity to seek and obtain further understanding of other subjects that were not studied at university or college. The capacity to understand gives personal contentment and social acceptance because it is only through understanding that we can deal with problems, adjust to new situations, and appreciate and be appreciated by other people. These are matters of attitudes, feelings, emotions and personal relationships that we stressed as important aims of higher education at the beginning of Chapter 2. It's impossible to prove, but let us at least suggest for your consideration, that people who have had a higher education are happier and more contented than those who have not.

Further Reading

Ellis, Walter. (1994) The Oxbridge conspiracy. Michael Joseph.
Hoggart, Richard. (1958) The uses of literacy. Penguin Books.
Paxman, Jeremy. (1990) Friends in high places. Michael Joseph.

6. Students in the System: access and participation

Introduction

Fees are one price to pay and, as we have seen, other sacrifices may be needed as part of a commitment to enter higher education. Getting in, and what you get out of it, depends not only on money but on the four As: ability, achievement, attitudes and aspirations. All of those will affect a person's decision to apply for entry; they will also affect decisions on whether they are admitted and, later, how well they succeed. This chapter deals with the size and shape of the system of provision and participation, and, particularly the process of entry and the nature of the student body.

I.   How many students are there?

To be blunt, nobody knows exactly. It is difficult to set criteria for who should be included in statistics given the diversity of study patterns. Do doctors on a week's professional updating course count as postgraduates? Do those pursuing high level NVQ qualifications by private study and work-based assessment of competence? This is one of the difficulties of comparison with other countries – one study in the early 1990s tried to present a pan-European picture and simply could not do so. It could not give an agreed total for UK polytechnics; it stated that there were no part-time students in several countries where our experience is that many students would be classified as part-time using UK norms. In many EU countries the discounts available to students, on travel, food, entertainment and so on are such that it is worth paying the nominal fee charged to register on a course… any course! In some countries there is no selection procedure – students who pass school leaving examinations have a right to enter university – but not vocational and professional colleges, many of which have a higher status than universities, another contrast with the UK.

However, there are official statistics and these, for l996-97, are shown in Table 6.1 – excluding over 1 million short-course students. The last figures, of course, depend on how knowledge is divided and categorised. Medicine and dentistry had just over 40,000 students but subjects allied to medicine – nursing, physiotherapy, psychiatry, biomedical sciences etc. had nearly 140,000 and that excluded some students in institutions funded by the Department of Health and not, then, under the 'official' umbrella of the Higher Education Statistics Agency. The establishment of HESA has helped statistics to be fuller and more reliable but not yet fully accurate. We still lack a lot of data, particularly about part-time students. Be careful when presented with statistics to know what population they are referring to. Many are cited as if they referred to all students when, for instance over social class, they refer only to full-time entrants through clearing houses because that information is only collected at that

total students	1,891,500	
of which	980,000	were female
	697,000	were part-time
	353,000	were post graduates
	211,000	were from overseas
of which	90,000	were from EU countries
	61,500	were from Commonwealth countries
nearly	1,300,000	were aged 21 or over
nearly	600,000	were aged 30 or over

The biggest subject groups were:

Combined general courses	296,000
Business and Finance	243,000

and the smallest

Veterinary Science, Agriculture etc.	19,300
Librarianship and Information Science	20,400

Table 6.1   Students in UK higher education 1996-7.

point. Others may use postal codes to impute a social class to students but that is not wholly reliable. Social class for students is, anyway, derived from their father's occupation – if half of them are over 21 when they enter, is what their father does relevant? One survey of Open University students showed a significant class 'shift' among students many of whom were using higher education to confirm their new class, not as a transition process to it, as may be the case for younger, full-time school leaver entrants.

II.   Getting in

This section mainly focuses on entrants to full-time undergraduate courses – degrees, HNDs etc. Selection for *part-time* courses is not systematic; in most cases, those who satisfy basic entry requirements will be offered a place, often without an interview. Where there is employer sponsorship, a positive reference will outweigh any marginal deficiencies in academic achievement. Entry to *postgraduate* courses is also locally organised with a wide variety of criteria applied. Here we are concerned with candidates through the clearing house – UCAS, the Universities and Colleges Admissions Service. Many of the statistics are taken from their report on those entering in 1997. Other systems, for courses for particular professions, are operated by UCAS, but they are tiny and marginal to this book's focus. UCAS publishes a "Parents' Guide" and a set of guidance handbooks for potential applicants on specific subject areas, as well as other reports in its area of interest.

For entry in 1997, 458,781 people made over 2 million applications. The form allows up to five choices and the average was 4.6 applications per person. Of those, 336,338 were offered and accepted a place, about 73%. Nearly 7,000 more were offered a place unconditionally but did not accept it. So, over 75% of applicants were 'acceptable'. The proportion of applicants gaining entry has risen slowly but steadily, in recent years. There is now, no formal national entry qualification, as there used to be – the diversity of qualifications available and the success on courses of experienced entrants without

Degree subject group	Appli-cations	Accept-ances	Ratio	Home acceptances		High Alevel scores	>5 H grades	BTEC SCOT-VEC	SNVQ GNVQ	Access Found-ation
				Men	Women					
A Medicine and dentistry	71,931	5,871	12.3:1	2477	2879	4018	429	4	2	16
B Subjects allied to medicine	164,959	19,575	8.4:1	5673	11806	1736	579	1380	798	1297
C Biological sciences	126,786	18,825	6.7:1	6086	10754	3131	463	501	327	1028
D Agriculture and related subjects	23,526	4,403	5.3:1	1006	1465	436	83	302	67	57
F Physical sciences	85,780	16,050	5.3:1	9550	5182	2928	370	368	177	464
G Mathematical sciences and informatics	124,591	24,638	5.1:1	13944	4060	2867	252	1216	1995	787
H/J Engineering and technology	134,754	26,033	5.2:1	14605	2396	2510	444	2144	566	383
K Architecture, building and planning	36,636	6,980	5.2:1	4033	1158	374	152	719	402	161
L/M Social Studies	251,474	40,443	6.2:1	14073	21125	6052	630	1232	1459	3198
N Business and administrative studies	271,335	42,048	6.5:1	14382	13798	1811	750	3018	4000	685
P Mass communications and documentation	59,113	8,381	7.1:1	2432	4060	354	40	1002	646	303
Q/R/T Languages and related disciplines	121,020	19,199	6.3:1	5199	12638	5579	178	169	73	804
V Humanities	63,221	11,076	5.7:1	4888	5757	2691	96	169	54	778
W Creative arts	168,584	29,041	5.8:1	9880	13200	1480	83	4072	1667	3273
X Education	113,159	13,168	8.6:1	2510	10281	363	158	1468	448	1243
Combined sciences	24,443	7,105	3.4:1	3652	2635	1225	170	362	157	246
Combined social studies	51,667	3,529	14.6:1	1522	1612	435	110	170	196	139
Combined arts	30,820	8,356	3.7:1	2476	5266	1169	134	298	103	657
Science plus social studies or arts	68,987	11,573	6.0:1	5329	4739	725	238	1005	682	593
Social studies combined with arts	65,354	9,477	6.9:1	3151	5137	1326	251	367	376	492
Other general and combined studies	43,038	10,567	4.1:1	3432	6255	579	225	811	606	1030
Total degree courses	**2,101,178**	**336,338**	**6.2:1**	**130,300**	**146,203**	**41,789**	**5,835**	**2,1783**	**13,785**	**17,624**
HND courses				16166	10649	14	16	4779	5549	1054

Table 6.2   Applications and acceptances via UCAS for 1997 entry.

'normal' academic qualifications has eroded that 'threshold' in practice. It is now a matter of local judgement over a person's 'ability to benefit'. Over 14,500 entrants in 1997 were classified as having no qualifications. Many selectors still do operate traditional baselines, but as guidance indicators on a student's chances of success on a course. It is worth noting that in Scotland, with a broader base of school study post-16 and entry possible with Higher qualifications at age 17 (or even 16), a higher proportion of the age group enter higher education, but a higher proportion do not get beyond the first year of study.

The competition for entry varies, as does the attitude to different qualifications. One in seven home students entering courses in business and administration had S/GINVQ qualifications; in Medicine there were only 2 in over 4,500; in Dentistry and Veterinary Science, none. In Veterinary Science, all but two of those entering with A Levels – 343 in all – had 26 points or more; that is, at least ABB. The Scots needed at least 5 Highers and 95% also had passes in the Certificate of Sixth Year Studies (CSYS).

Table 6.2 summarises a complex picture. It gives, for degree courses in the UCAS clusters:

- the total number of applications – not applicants, who usually make five applications each.
- the number of acceptances
- the ratio of the first to the second. Where this is under 5:1 it suggests that people have been accepted on to courses for which they did not, at first, apply, but have re-routed during clearing.
- The number of UK students accepted, by gender and then within those, the numbers with:
  – high A Level scores – 26 or more in three subjects
  – 6 or more H grades
  – BTEC or SCOTVEC qualification
  – S/G/NVQs
  – Access or foundation courses.

This tries to show those clusters where high-grade qualifications are essential, and those where a more diverse entry pattern prevails. There are variations within clusters – chemistry, geography and environmental science are all in cluster F, but have different patterns. The UCAS report gives detailed figures. There will also be differences across institutions in the degree of competition and general attitude towards the diversity of possible pathways into higher education. Advanced GNVQs are new qualifications but have gained acceptability in modern universities committed to access – indeed one study by UCAS shows that those studying such courses are very slightly more likely to be made an offer than the average for all applicants – 93.5% compared to 92% for 1997 entry. The commitment of institutions to expand is shown in the figures from that same study. The percentage of applicants made at least one offer is shown in Table 6.3.

Year of Entry	Percentage of applicants with one or more offers
1994	76.0
1995	86.5
1996	88.4
1997	92.0

Table 6.3   Applicants offered a place.

III.   A closer look at a varied picture

The figures you have seen show that higher education is very diverse. Many people still have an image of universities as being mainly for middle-class school leavers with academic qualifications studying full-time on campus. Things have changed. This section looks more closely at what kind of people students are - their backgrounds and characteristics, - and it debates some of the issues raised.

1.   Social Class

Full time degree students tend to come disproportionately from the middle and professional classes. Figure 6.4 gives figures for entrants in 1994 compared to the total *economically active* population. Children of unemployed or retired parents are not classifiable. Figure 6.5 then gives figures home acceptances to full-time courses in 1997 against four clusters of ethnic origin. In all cases the percentage of acceptances from the 'upper' social class groups is marginally higher than the percentage of applicants.

In 1995, the Age Participation Index (API) – the percentage of young people going into *full-time* higher education – was 45% of the 'top' three classes, 15% of the other three. This gap of 3:1 had narrowed from 5:1 in 1980, 6:1 in 1970, 7:1 in 1960. In 1940 it had been 5.5:1. The class structure of society as a whole has changed substantially over those years. Researchers put the closing of the gap down to rising aspirations and so a greater tendency to apply, fuelled by increased qualification rates at school level and access courses thereafter.

2.   Ethnic minorities

Students from ethnic minorities are better represented in higher education than whites. In 1994 12.2% of young people in higher education were non-white whereas the age group as a whole had only 7.3%. This over representation is true for all ages. Students from black groups tend to be older. This is less true of Asians and others. The proportion of students from ethnic minorities had been increasing steadily until the atypical 1997 entry when there was a 'boom' of 70,000 extra entrants after the introduction of fees from 1998 was announced.

Applicants from men are a significant majority of those from Pakistani or Bangladeshi backgrounds. Those from women dominate the Black Caribbean group. From the Indian, Chinese and Black African groups the figures are more evenly balanced.

Students from ethnic minorities are roughly twice as likely to enter post-1992

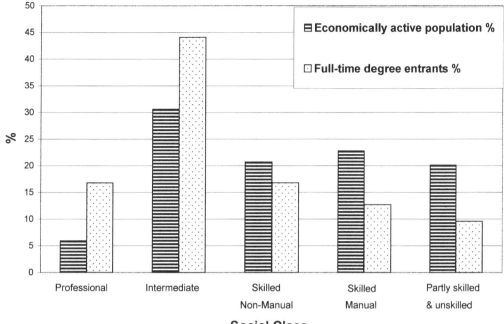

Figure 6.4   Full time entrants by class compared to the population as a whole.

		White	**Black**	**Asian**	**Other**
1	**Professional**	14	8	10	16
2	**Intermediate**	42	31	27	35
3N	**Skilled Non-manual**	13	18	12	13
3M	**Skilled Manual**	15	10	19	12
4	**Partly skilled**	7	10	12	8
5	**Unskilled**	2	2	6	2

Table 6.5   Home acceptances, 1997 entry, by ethnic origin and social class.

universities and colleges rather than universities existing before 1992. This is partly a result of the highly competitive courses they apply for at the traditional universities.

3.   Age

There are differences between the two former sectors in terms of ages of all students. In 1996 68% of students aged under 19 were in pre-1992 universities whilst 63% and 65% of 19-24 year-olds and those over 25 were in 1992 universities. Again, this is partly a function of the courses offered. The courses with the highest percentage of students aged 25 or over accepted via UCAS in 1997 are shown in Table 6.6. most of those are areas where the modern universities are strong or where there is a strong commitment within them to wider access.

	%
Other general and combined studies (mainly modular schemes)	22.5
Education	20.4
Subjects allied to medicine	16.2
Social studies	16.0
Combined arts	15.9
Humanities	15.7

Table 6.6.   Subjects with the highest percentage of students aged 25 or more.
Source: UCAS Statistics for 1997.

4.   Disability

Disability is a delicate and difficult topic because it relies on self-declaration. Of all first year students in 1996 across all modes of study, some 14,800 out of 570,000 declared a disability, but 182,000 were classified as 'not known'. The average of those on whom information was held was 3.8%, higher among full-timers than part-timers. The biggest cluster of disabilities in both groups related to diabetes, epilepsy and asthma. For full-timers this was followed by dyslexia, for part-timers by mobility difficulties.

5.   Where do students come from?

Table 6.1 showed that there were over 200,000 students studying at higher education level in the UK but who were normally resident outside the country. There are thousands more studying in their own countries but on courses leading to the award of a UK university and with some teaching by staff of UK universities. The examinations of these students are usually controlled by the 'home' university. The most active university in this field is the Open University which has study centres in many cities on the European mainland. Its materials for management courses have been translated into several languages including Russian and those of other Eastern European countries.

Where universities validate programmes in other countries there has recently been concern over control of quality and standards. There are also issues of differences across cultures. In many Asian countries knowledge, transmitted by experts, is seen by many students as unchallengeable whereas within the UK there is a spirit of greater challenge and criticism. Some concepts do not translate easily. For example, the language of local self-management is new within former state bureaucracies. The place of the individual in the group or wider society is different in, say, China from in the U.K. The 'normal' attitudes to women, children, the family and many moral and social issues can differ widely from country to country as well as among individuals.

Ironically, it costs the UK to have students from the developed countries of the European Union - about £100m per year was a recent estimate. In part that had been because more students enter the country on exchange schemes than go the other way - the language barrier and cultural attitudes affect that. Another part lies in the treaties on mobility where EU students in any EU country have the same rights as students who are natives of that country. So, Finnish students, for example, count as UK students when government funding allocations are made. There was a large inflow of

Irish students into Northern Ireland when the south had fees and the north did not; now the flow has stopped and reversed. The largest group of EU students in the UK is from Greece where the system of higher education is relatively less well developed. The expansion of the EU to the east may prompt a further review of fees and student support by the UK government.

There are interesting patterns of movement within the UK. Part-time students are, of course, bound to their locality. The majority of full-time students don't travel far. They study at university or college in their own region or the one or two next to it. There are two places where the balance of movement is very one sided.

In Scotland many go to their local institution and 78% of full-time UK entrants to Scottish universities were from within Scotland. Over 6,000 students came to Scotland from elsewhere including over 1600 from Northern Ireland. That figure may change sharply if other UK students have to pay a year's extra fee to Scottish universities when Scottish students do not - an anomaly in the 1998 legislation on higher education. On the other hand, lees than 2,500 Scots went elsewhere.

For Northern Ireland the position is even more extreme. Only 10 new students went there in 1997 from the rest of the UK! Over 4000 'crossed the water' to Scotland and England, with a few to Wales. So, over 98% of full-time students in Northern Ireland are 'local'. Hidden behind that is a religious difference - protestants are more likely to leave; catholics more likely to stay.

IV.   The benefits from accepting overseas students
1.   Cultural diversity
Bringing these diverse cultures together on a course enriches the experience of all. Any one view can be tested against others. Many UK students are parochial in their world view (though not as bad as many in the USA!). The level of discourse on world events is, in our experience, much more sophisticated amongst those from the European mainland. The British have a reputation for tolerance and pluralism. Higher education provides a place where these can be developed. There is a risk, of course, of 'cultural imperialism' - a belief that 'our' way is best and should be adopted by everybody (again, the USA is worse), but that is slowly fading as the former British Empire fades into history. It can be healthy, too, to have people comment on the beggars on city streets, the civil war in Northern Ireland (not just 'troubles') and other issues - to see ourselves as others see us.

2.   Financial
Students from outside the EU pay 'full' fees, so that higher education makes a profit out of them. The calculation is that a trip to a higher education 'fair' in, say, Kuala Lumpur is justified even if only 2 or 3 students enrol as a result. Over a three year programme they would each pay over £15,000 in fees whilst the extra cost of teaching them in a group that already exists is marginal. When high fees were first introduced by the Thatcher administration, there were even 'ghetto' courses created exclusively for full fee students from overseas. With the problems in the Asian economies, numbers may fall and several universities with large student populations from those countries

will have problems balancing their budgets. Many have reduced fees from countries hard hit by currency devaluations.

3.   Research contribution

Overseas students are essential to the research efforts of higher education. In 1996-97 over one-third of all full-time postgraduate students were from overseas, most paying full fees. Many projects particularly in the sciences, could not proceed without their contribution.

4.   Potential international influence

On return to their country students often move quickly to positions of influence. If they are in trade and industry, or particularly in government, their attitudes to economic cooperation with the UK can be affected by their experience as a student and a visitor. So can their attitudes to political issues dealt with internationally, such as treaties on the environment, UN resolutions on human rights etc. There may, then, be benefit to the UK balance of payments, or to contracts giving work to UK citizens. If they become academics, links between institutions may be enhanced as part of the perceived need for higher education to be international. At the least, there can be an impressive list of such linkages in publicity material.

5.   An intellectual resource

Some may stay. Their periods as students can be seen as an extended selection process whereby UK universities cream off the best brains of other countries so enhancing their competitive position.

There are moral issues there, of course. The British Empire had a history of exploiting less developed countries; some UK companies still do. In the light of that, and our privileged position in the world there is an argument of duty to help the less fortunate countries. The level the UK invests in international aid is below the norm established by the United Nations. Further work through higher education would be one way of redressing that balance.

V.   Are there too many students?

When the Robbins Committee, in 1963, anticipated growth in student numbers, there were cries of 'more will mean worse'. At that time about 6% of school leavers went on to university or college, full-time. Some people claimed that that represented the whole of the 'pool of ability' of those capable of pursuing degree level work. Now the figure is about 30% and if we add on people who go later, or who go part-time, about half the population, by age 35, will have had higher education of some sort. Already in Scotland over half of any age cohort of women go on, full-time, before they are 21. In 1963 under one quarter of an age group passed the 11+ exam.

At the same time as numbers have expanded, the degree class normally achieved has moved from lower second to upper second. So, more students are getting in, and are achieving better results. And that is despite significant reductions in cost. There is conflicting evidence about consistency of standards over time, and comparisons are difficult because of the changing base of knowledge, and the introduction of more varied assessment methods that test more abilities than the good short-term memory and speed writing skills essential to traditional exams.

The doubling of student numbers in the 1990s has been driven from the supply side since universities' income depended on student numbers and increased income depended on growth. That incentive will continue and the next few years will see bigger cohorts of 18 year-olds before that demographic trend flattens out. There has been, however, for three years, a reduction in the proportion of students, especially boys, who stay on in education, in England, after the age of 16, after a long period when staying on became much more common. That could mean a smaller proportion of the age group will try for higher education so that a 'natural' level of demand will emerge. This may fluctuate according to circumstances but we suggest that a new 'plateau' may have been reached that will operate for the next decade. There will, in that period, be more places on offer than are filled, particularly in sciences and engineering. The introduction of fees, and the abolition of grants will affect domestic demand; the strong pound and the world-wide economic crisis will affect overseas demand. There may, in time, be another surge, as sophisticated knowledge, understanding and skills become even more important in the 'information' society predicted for us. Certainly we see continued growth of postgraduate study and professional (re)development as people need to learn, to cope with change.

At the same time, despite growth in numbers, employers report difficulties in recruiting the right kind of graduate. In some cases, this is subject specific, such as in engineering and computing. The slight recent resurgence of the study of maths and science in schools may, in the longer term, help redress this. Some professions, such as nursing, that have moved to expect entrants to have gone through some form of higher education, may need to review their entry qualifications, or salary levels, to be able to attract sufficient numbers. There are graduates who are unemployed, and others who are under-employed in their jobs. Perhaps, then, the *general* level of supply of graduates is at a satisfactory level. There are two views here. Employers claim that the general skills of graduate applicants are not at a level they expect from people with a degree; yet sgraduates in employment complain that their graduate level competencies are not used to the full by employers. Both may be right.

With recent expansion we now produce as many graduates per 1,000 people as other developed countries, and more than most other countries in the EU. Where there does seem to be agreement is that, relative to other countries, the UK has a skills shortage at intermediate levels - the higher technician grades. The place of HND qualifications in any expansion or the fuller use of a pass degree as a step-off point, as in Scotland, is now an issue for debate. The expansion of HE within FE colleges, recommended by the Dearing Committee, may be one approach to this rebalancing within the higher education pattern of participation, with the number of students at postgraduate level also expanding – there are already more such than there were undergraduates 30 years ago.

VI.   What are students like?

A survey of children in Lancaster showed that an abiding image of students at the university was that they ate green apples! This obviously showed sophistication in moving beyond the red, shining sweet norm of childhood. Other images through the media can show greater childishness (Winnie-the-Pooh Societies), charitableness (community action), concern (in protests about the environment or the ethics of some animal research), quirkiness (in Rag Weeks) or even conservative quaintness (May Balls and punting on the river).

Interviews with finalists in traditional universities by High Fliers Research for Channel 4 showed that *on average*, they studied 28 hours a week in addition to attending lectures, small groups and laboratory classes. Only 14% went to the cinema or theatre once a week, but 84% went to a pub and 47% went to a club. In the week before the survey, nearly 60% had drunk wine, with similar figures for lager and spirits. More (40%) drank bottled beer than draft bitter (26%). Over 25% used the Internet at least daily and 68% at least once a week.

As a life objective, 'living life to the full' at 77% was a long way ahead of the second-ranking 'being secure financially' at 55% (most of them came from middle class backgrounds). The next on the list were 'an exciting social life' (49%) 'a successful career' (45%), marriage and a family (31%) and ' world travel' 30%. 'Contributing to society' got only 26% from these children of the Thatcher years.

Their heroes were Richard Branson and Nelson Mandela. The Spice Girls and Jeremy Beadle topped the list of those not to be stuck in a lift with (though the Spice Girls were ranked 8th in the preferred company for an evening). 'Friends' and 'Eastenders' were way ahead of any other favourite TV programme with Radio 1 attracting nearly 70% and Radio 3 only 3% (Radio 2 got only 2%, but Classic FM hit 10%). They read broadsheet newspapers led by 'The Times' (34%) 'Guardian' and (23%) with 'The Independent' close to 'The Daily Telegraph' at 18% and 19% respectively.

So, those students were pretty mainstream. In politics (New) Labour led with 34% with Lib.Dems on 22% and Conservatives on 16%. Over 20% 'did not know' which suggests that any intellect or analytical abilities are not directed at politics. 'Work hard, play hard' was the summary; but the image of activists from the 1960s is dead. A closer summary is 'self-indulgent apathy on social issues'.

Are they intellectual? With over 30% of the age group now entering higher education before the age of 35 they may be above average intelligence, but most will not be at an extreme. Anyone hoping to go up to college and spend time with quality minds in intense debate is likely to be disappointed. More and more, students are seen as instrumental in their objectives, determined to work within the course framework which they see as setting boundaries to what is necessary not as a base for exploring further. A pity, since this period, especially for young, full-time students should be a time of exploration of oneself and one's world, looking for insights from a range of sources and developing skills of independence of mind and competence in learning for the rest of life. There are even research reports of younger students resenting mature colleagues in seminars who ask questions and challenge. In so doing they stop the tutor delivering an uninterrupted message for the students to write down and, later, repeat.

VII.   Local differences

This chapter has referred to the student population as a whole, or to large sub-sets within it. We must stress that the 'local' picture of particular universities or colleges can be very different. We have noted some differences across the four countries of the UK. Because of its size, England makes a contribution that dominates any 'average' figure for the UK as a whole. Two more examples from Scotland will emphasise this. In England in 1996, about 12% of higher education students were in further education colleges. In Scotland, in 1996, one third of the full-time new undergraduate entrants went into further education colleges, and over three-quarters of the part-timers did. In England the proportion of 18-21 year-olds going in to full-time higher education is the lowest of the four countries of the UK - about 30%, with the proportion of men and women being much the same. In Scotland in 1996 the figure was nearly 47%, with men at 41% and women at nearly 53%.

If countries are different, institutions within countries or even in the same city are different. Modern universities with their commitment to inclusiveness and access have, roughly, twice as many students from ethnic minorities as traditional ones. In London, in two cases, students from minority groups make up the majority of the student body. At Leeds Metropolitan University there are thousands of part-time undergraduates whilst at Leeds University there are only hundreds. The London School of Economics has a near majority of its students from overseas. And the examples could be extended. Edinburgh, Heriot Watt and Napier are three very different places in the same city and in Northern Ireland the two universities are very different as a matter of policy, set when the Chilver Report helped to establish the University of Ulster.

Departments and courses within institutions are also different - think of sociology and engineering as stereotypical contrasts. Certain types of students are drawn to the one rather than the other and entrants to any course will find people like themselves on it. They will establish peer friendship groups and patterns of existence that they are comfortable with. Most will have little awareness of, or contact with, other academic areas of the university. One reason for this is the layout of campuses. They are big and students don't vary their the patterns of movement within them very much. They may go to the department, library, refectory, bar and bus stop. That is why the Student Union is so important: across the bridge table, in the hang gliding society or the choir there is a mix across the disciplines. This is where different world views, conditioned by disciplines, can meet. The relative importance of aesthetics, order and precision, moral values, imagination, economic relevance, methods of enquiry, cultural perspectives, can be discussed and different perspectives be recognised as legitimate – different, but equally valid.

VIII.   The Admissions process
1.   The Clearing House system
As we have noted, applications for full-time undergraduate study are made through a clearing house. Why? The simple answer is efficiency and its benefits, mainly for the institutions. UCCA handled its first intake for 1963 as a way of coping with large numbers of applicants some of whom made multiple applications and then held offers

from several places. The institutions, before that, did not know how many of the people they were expecting would show up to register. There was also a penalty for some applicants, placed on a waiting list because courses were apparently full when some places were earmarked for people who would go elsewhere, because they were keeping their options open and had not kept institutions fully informed of their decisions on offers from elsewhere.

Numbers are now much higher; pressures on staff in institutions are greater – the demands of research assessment, and of teaching audits as well as much higher staff:student ratios. A standardised, closed system, easy to operate with a minimum of time spent on 'phantom' applicants is, therefore, desirable. That is what UCAS offers.

The disciplines of the system are part of this – the early formal closing date, the prescribed times within which offers and replies should be made, the and reduction in informal entry routes, give a security and clarity on both sides. There is the potential for a watchdog role to detect any allegations of bias (as in racially based selection by some medical schools in the 1980s), and a systematic base for statistics to monitor trends and to help plan policy and provision. At a local level, it allows those responsible for admissions to courses to find the 'right' threshold level of offer against mainstream qualifications that will get the number of students they want. Tutors for less popular courses can then pitch their offer to optimise acceptances, and can do this in the light of knowledge about the typical offer levels of the other courses applied for. This can, of course, lead to playing games, but it is an open game.

There is a consequential benefit for applicants. They can know what kind of grades will be needed normally to get into any course and so can choose their five for the form in relation to a – realistic! – assessment of what they are likely to get. The figures we gave earlier on acceptability of Vocational Qualifications are one example of this.

There are disadvantages, mainly for applicants, and their advisers. The early closing date means choices are made a year before they become operational. This is usually before any visits to institutions, so decisions may be based on inadequate information. It is usually before 'mock' exams, so a realistic assessment of final performance is difficult. Adult students doing a one year course in further education will hardly be known to their tutors and may be unsure of their own likely levels of performance. Once the choices are made, and forms submitted, there are inflexibilities that make it difficult to cope with change of mind, or with better decisions based on fuller information. One officer used to talk of 'bureaucratic bluffs' to deter students, who changed their mind, from changing their decisions. Things have much improved with the merger of several previous clearing houses and under the leadership of Tony Higgins, the UCAS chief executive.

Nevertheless, the advantage of having a clear position, on both sides, by late spring in the year of entry is off-set by lack of provision for a 'pre-clearing' second round. The rush after exam results are published is well administered (more easily for Scots whose Higher results come a month before A Levels; less easily for those with vocational qualifications some of which publish results later). Whether it is the best way for students is doubtful. The drop out and failure rate for those admitted during clearing is higher, and not only because such entrants tend to have lower qualifications. A year out would be a better option for many of them. A good, later decision is better than a quick bad one. Many such students, having dropped out, return later and study something different successfully. Even many graduates, with the knowledge of hindsight, say they took the 'wrong' subject.

Discussions are under way to devise a system where applications are considered from any candidate only after their results are known. Meanwhile, people who are not happy with their projected pathway after the admissions system has processed them by, say, May or June, should explore what can be done. UCAS will advise on how to work the system and most admissions tutors are humane and sympathetic. If you reach an agreement with a course tutor outside the formal system, this can be, then, incorporated into that system. The advice is: don't give up, be polite but persistent, and get agreements in writing.

2.   Decision criteria

The reasons behind students' choice of courses are many and varied. The universities in Newcastle reckoned that Alan Shearer's transfer from Blackburn was worth several thousand extra applications. Many criteria are not academic, but can relate to family or friendly connections, geographical location, or comparative costs of living. The decision processes by staff in universities and colleges are also varied. People bring their personalities, prejudices and preferences to decisions. There is, though, a more limited framework for decisions.

How, then, does the process work? What are the important factors? Here are three main models.

In the first, most decisions are made in a central unit. Courses will have 'standard' offers for candidates with 'standard' qualifications. Administrative staff will home in on what applicants are studying or have studied. They will then make the offer, conditional or unconditional, and refer to academic staff only those that fall outside guidelines. At the time of an offer an invitation may also go out to attend an open day when more information can be gained to help the decision as to whether to accept the offer. This is a low-level selling process, dealing with applicants on a group batch-process basis. There is probably a lowish acceptance rate, at least as first choice, but the institutions believe that a candidate's 'pecking order' of preferences has been decided at the start of the process and can be affected only marginally, if at all. So, they offer a friendly responsiveness when students approach them but otherwise aim at efficient processing with a high level of 'redundancy'. That is, many applicants processed will not accept offers, but this is acceptable because not a lot of effort has been spent on individuals as part of the group processes at, for example, the open day.

The second model involves academic staff making judgements on individuals, but still based only on the application form, but on more of the data it gives. Once qualifications are scrutinised, other factors may play a part in decisions on those who hover on the offer/reject threshold. The number of people rejected may be higher than in the first group, but more often, an offer may be made at a level such that the candidate will not accept so that the psychology of the shared decision will be different. A selector will look first at qualifications already achieved. For many school students this will mean passes at GCSE or Standard grade. A good spread with good grades gets you through this first stage.

Then, do the subjects currently being studied form an acceptable mix for the course? Maths and physics may be seen as essential for engineering (though one may suffice in some places). Chemistry *or* biology can substitute for one another for biochemistry, or even biology itself. For law, some tutors do not like A Level Law because, they claim, they have to re-educate those who've studied it!

Projected grades will be the next stop, even though those are notoriously unreliable. Much will depend on whether the tutor knows the school from past applicants – likely in Scotland and Northern Ireland where recruitment is more local.

The same is true of the reference. Even for school students this need not be the headteacher or careers tutor or head of sixth form. Some references show obvious prejudice – favourable or not. Some are bland, standard statements. One school we knew simply provided an overall grade of potential to succeed – from A to E – with no other comment. It is likely that tutors will give more weight to the small space allocated to applicants to express themselves and to favour those who are articulate and show they have a balanced, active life, perhaps with something that suggests an attractive eclecticism rather than anorak nerdishness.

The third model brings in the interview. Interviews are expensive for both candidates and staff, so they are used less and less. Most staff are not trained interviewers and so don't make good use of them as devices for discrimination between otherwise equal candidates. Interviews are still used for courses where entry is highly competitive, or where the course leads to professional qualifications, especially those which involve close work in serving people – medicine, education, social work. The selection criteria here will also involve evidence of relevant work experience whether it is working in a chemist's shop, teaching at Sunday School or doing voluntary work in a shelter for the homeless. This not only shows commitment but is likely to have brought candidates closer to the realities of life after graduation and so suggests their application has idealism tempered with realism.

Interviews will also test how far applicants have exaggerated in their personal statements. A claim to an interest in 'science fiction' may prompt questions that go beyond 'Star Trek', H.G. Wells or even Isaac Asimov. The questions for which answers should be prepared include: 'Why this subject?' and 'Why here?' Answers should show some research and argument for the decisions, which should be the student's own, not 'because I was advised to by teacher, parent etc.' There may also be questions about recent reading or current affairs to test how rounded a world view a potential student has. Good self-presentation is what is wanted – appearance and articulateness, though some allowances are made for appearance. There should be a spark of difference, of originality, even of challenge, provided a view can be defended, not just asserted. All of these factors will be considered by a tutor, who will also be looking to get a varied group, so that people will challenge one another and develop the debate and disputation that lie at the heart of the best higher education.

7.   Ways of Learning

A student's job is to learn. But how? All students arrive with some skills in how to learn, but they're not always appropriate. This chapter looks at why. It tries to give an understanding of what is required and why some students find learning easier than others. The way students learn depends partly on their schooling, their temperament, and how they were brought up. Every student has a different background and we can't describe them all. So we'll sketch a couple of contrasting characters. The sketches are caricatures. As caricatures, they may seem judgmental and unfairly critical. They're not supposed to be. Indeed, the message we want to get across is the need to be understanding.

I.   Understanding why students behave as they do

The two students are Kim and Robin. Kim is just as often male as female and Robin is more often male, but it is easier to distinguish one from the other if I write as if they are of different sexes. Kim is a little dependent and conformist, whilst Robin is more independent.

Kim had a conventional middle-class upbringing. She is quiet and conscientious. Her parents are not reckless, spontaneous or humorous in personal relations. They are a little tense and a bit formal. Kim is a product of the Protestant ethic:- she works hard and does not spend money freely because she is not given much by her parents. She has not been told to go to church regularly. She does so because that is the thing to do. She has accompanied her family to church for as long as she can remember. Since before she first went to school, her parents and her church have provided a consistent moral authority. For Kim, matters of right and wrong are not open matters. They have correct answers. Reference to the Bible, convention, parents or other established authorities provides guidance when an individual is uncertain. But there is no uncertainty in reality; all is clear so long as you know.

Unlike Kim, Robin experienced inconsistent values. When, before the age of 5, he did something wrong in the morning, Mum would threaten that Dad would tan his backside when he came home that evening. But if Robin was a good boy in the afternoon, Mum would forget about that. So what his parents said was not consistent. The rules were varying all the time. Because one day was different from another, Robin soon learned to be constantly testing to find out what he could get away with. So Robin learned to be an opportunist. He acquired quick judgement in sizing up a situation. His behaviour was governed less by rules, than by expediency and what was practical at the time.

1.   Experience at school

It was the same when they went to school. Kim soon discovered that all the authorities agreed. Both her parents, the teachers and the textbooks all agreed about what was true and what was not true. Her job was to learn it. So learning was a process of collecting facts and memorising them. For this she was well rewarded with adult approval. Basically, Kim had a very secure environment and people were tender-hearted towards her.

Robin's experience was very different. He continually created situations in which power had to be exerted. Every teacher has met Robin. He was always testing the limits of the implicit rules laid down by the teachers. When the class was told to be quiet, he would whisper to his neighbour. The teacher would ignore it and Robin would feel able to whisper a little louder. This process would go on until the teacher felt his authority was being challenged. Then Robin had to be checked or punished. That meant that the relationship between Robin and his teachers was more tough than tender, and more to do with compulsion than caring. He never had security. He was always being repressed and sooner or later his repressed feelings would emerge as aggression. That aggression might be expressed acceptably in sport, less acceptably in poking fun at other pupils and teachers, or unacceptably in more misbehaviour. Misbehaviour simply provoked a vicious circle with the teachers becoming more and more short-tempered and punitive towards him. Robin learned to live by his wits and by expediency because, in spite of outward appearances, he had never had a stable relationship to rely on.

However, the rules at school were more consistent than at home. Robin gradually learned to play the school game by the school rules. True, he continued to transgress more often than Kim, and because of his reputation, he was not so easily forgiven. He continued to experience more punishments than she. Nonetheless, to a very large extent, the school provided some stability for Robin. Without it he might have tried some petty pilfering and got on the wrong side of the law. Robin progressed academically because he feared failure and punishment; while Kim progressed because she tried to do her best all the time. Robin tried to minimise failure. Kim tried to maximise achievement. So Robin did as little as possible to get by. You might think that, in contrast, Kim went beyond the call of duty, but she soon learned that that was a mistake.

Psychologically speaking, enterprise in learning was punished. When she showed initiative and produced ideas and information with which her teachers were not familiar, they felt insecure. For example, when learning about ants, she discovered from an encyclopaedia at home that ants have an enemy that sprays acid at them. On volunteering this information in class, the biology teacher reacted with mild aggression by questioning her more deeply, saying, 'What do you know about that?' and 'You don't need to know about that yet'. The teacher felt threatened because he had only prepared a lesson on ants, not on their enemies.

Restricting her knowledge to that prescribed by those with power over her, threatened no one in authority and all were rewarded with the security that comes from not considering awkward questions. Limiting her memory to the facts prescribed by the teachers was always adequate to gain high marks and to earn the warm approval of both teachers and her parents. Education was a process of memorising the established facts and regurgitating them when required, particularly in examinations and tests.

Unlike Kim, Robin found that the easiest way to get by was not to sit down and try to remember all the facts in splendid isolation, but to try to understand how they were linked together. So although Robin learned less, he understood it better. At first, understanding and connecting one thing with another was not rewarded very much, but as he worked his way up the secondary school, this learning strategy began to pay off. So it was that, although pupils like Robin are the scourge of their teachers when lower down the school, and those without much ability leave at the age of 16, those with some ability obtain GCSEs good enough to enter the sixth form. Robin was made a school prefect, partly because it was expedient for the teachers to have him on their side in the war against indiscipline; and partly because he played rugby well and that was seen as leadership.

Kim was not regarded by her teachers as unimaginative and having no other interests than her school work because she sang in the school choir and was a member of the Christian Union. In the choir, she learned to sing a fraction of a second after everyone else so that if she made a mistake it would not be noticed. In the Christian Union, she learned to observe discussions without ever actually taking part. She thereby safely avoided any need to justify an opinion. This masterly avoidance of anything controversial, or of making any contribution at all, was later so well developed for use in university seminars, that she was in danger of becoming conspicuously inconspicuous. Because she was conscientious, did her best and did as she was told, Kim was regarded as a sound, but not outstanding, pupil academically. Because she never caused any trouble, her teachers steadily came to regard her as a good pupil. Good pupils are likely to succeed and success meant eventually going to university as they had done. Indeed the expectation of higher education had unwittingly been planted in her mind by the age of 13 or 14.

Because of the limitations of the school timetable, it was at that age that both she and Robin found it necessary to specialise in some subjects. Now pupils like Kim are less likely to opt for science subjects than languages, humanities and the social sciences. This is because it may be beyond the ability of a conscientious pupil to do well in mathematics, but a conscientious pupil will always get reasonable marks in arts subjects, such as history, geography and English. So when her parents looked at her end of term reports, the prospect of sixth form studies in pure and applied mathematics, physics and computing looked unwise. On the other hand, Robin, never one to sit over books for a long time, much preferred practical classes in science.

When they reached the sixth form, both Kim and Robin worked very hard, under pressure from both their teachers and their parents, to get good enough grades to enter higher education. Entry is highly competitive.

2.   The experience of higher education

When he arrived at university, Robin experienced the "decompression syndrome". His previous life had consisted almost entirely of two social worlds: school and home. Suddenly, in a matter of weeks, both these were removed. Whoopee! Gone were the pressures to conform. Gone were the pressures to work. He had achieved his recent goals to pass A Levels and enter higher education. He had not yet acquired new ones.

His parents were no longer there to insist that he did his homework before doing other things. In his first week, the Freshers' week, all the clubs and societies of the Students' Union put on displays to tempt him to join. He joined five, one for each weekday evening, and on Saturday, there was sport in the afternoon and a disco in the evening. On Saturday and Sunday mornings, he tended to sleep in so that the remainder of Sunday was the only time when he could work without feeling that in a short while, he must get up and go to some other activity. In fact his first week at university set his lifestyle for most of the next three years.

At first, it didn't seem to matter very much. The lecturers were not asking him to hand in work tomorrow. Because the syllabuses of the various A Level examining boards were different, some of the first year courses repeated work he had done at school. With his self-confident extravert nature and his ability to think quickly on his feet, he was quite vocal in tutorials and only his most perceptive tutors realised that he was not doing much work. In fact just over half his seminars and tutorials were led by postgraduate research students (though it would have been more like a quarter if he had gone to a 1992 university). In laboratories and other practical classes around 20% of his contacts were with postgraduates, and they were insufficiently experienced to be perceptive.

For Kim, it was different. She did not experience "decompression" because she kept the pressure on herself. She was self-disciplined. Her conscience was well developed. However, because her teachers had not given her homework to be handed in next week, she was not certain exactly what to do. One tutor had not told her anything; another had given her a bibliography a page long and she didn't know where to start. At school, she only had four books in that subject and they lasted the whole year. With the guidance of the teacher, she had worked steadily through them gathering information and noting it as she went. She realised that at university she would not have the close supervision of her teachers. At university you have to be more independent, but she assumed that independence meant doing the same thing without the close supervision. After all, that is the way she had been taught to study. Taking notes from lectures was much the same. At school, she was given guidance in what to note; notes were sometimes almost dictated. She saw that she now had the responsibility to select what she noted. This made her a little anxious because she might miss some important item of knowledge. The obvious thing was to play it safe and note as much as she could. As the weeks passed, her files of notes grew steadily thicker and she eyed them with a sense of achievement. For there, in those folders, was her knowledge.

Kim never discussed her work with other students. Why should she? She never did at school. In fact, talking in class was strongly discouraged there, and when else could you talk about your work? It was the same at university. "You shouldn't talk in lectures and it's difficult in the library". Her friends on the same corridor in the hall of residence did not take the same subject. She met people taking the same course in her department, but there was neither time nor place there to permit lengthy or profound discussion. For a long time, Kim didn't realise that discussion is an important part of student life. She thought discussion simply wasted time better spent in reading. After all, she had heard students on "University Challenge" say they are "reading" for a degree.

Robin, on the other hand, went to the Union bar both at lunchtime and in the evening. There he would talk about all manner of subjects with students from many different disciplines. He developed opinions about society and politics as well as discussing wide-ranging scientific and cultural issues that set his honours course in a wider context. Robin was getting quite a different kind of education. He was getting through a number of girl-friends too. And he was also getting addicted to alcohol. In later life, this damaged his liver and made him put on weight, but, for the moment, it showed more in his bank balance than his health and he worked some of it off in his sporting life.

Paradoxically, the personality characteristics of both Kim and Robin favour the subjects they chose not to do at the age of 13. Kim's conformity is quite acceptable in science, medicine and engineering; while, at the Union Bar, Robin acquires the breadth, independence and argumentative skill that is advantageous in the arts and social sciences.

3.   Implications for academic style and academic work

It is the purpose of higher education to change people, or more precisely, for them to change themselves. So if Kim and Robin were to stay as they were when they arrived, their higher education would have failed.

If students like Kim don't develop more independence of mind, they get low marks for their assignments, become anxious and depressed, try to work yet harder, and then overwork so that their minds become dulled rather than sparkling. In short, they get in a vicious circle of low academic confidence, overwork and excessive fatigue, leading to poor performance and even less academic confidence. If it is the purpose of higher education to broaden their outlook, to encourage original thinking, to challenge traditional beliefs, to practise the arts of criticism, to provide a meeting of lively minds, ... students like Kim have a long way to develop when they first arrive at university. When Kim first arrived, she didn't have a lively mind; and she sought the security of a few like-minded friends. She was unconsciously afraid that originality would disturb the values, relationships and support of her family and throw an unwanted and unaccustomed spotlight on her private thoughts.

That is not to say that Kim didn't have some very fine qualities when she first arrived in higher education. She was very reliable, hard working and unambitious. She was scrupulously honest. She would not object to monotonous tasks and any company that might have employed her would have got good value for low wages. But in higher education those qualities are not enough.

In practice most students like Kim do use their time in higher education to explore ideas, values and personalities they would not have experienced at home. If, during her second year, you see Kim untidily dressed with her arm slung round the waist of the long-haired drummer of a local band, perhaps you should sigh with satisfaction that she is growing up normally.

If, in his first year, Robin does not learn to take more responsibility, organise himself, plan his use of time, use the academic as well as the social resources of his institution, heed his longer term priorities and discipline himself to concentrate at his desk, he may fail his first year exams and drop out of university altogether. Compared with other students, he has always taken risks and lived for the present; but higher education is a long-term investment. He needs to recognise that the risks are greater now and there is not always someone at hand to protect him from his lack of self-discipline.

That is not to say that Robin's first year would have been wasted if he had dropped out. That is a common misconception and can give an unnecessary sense of failure. He matured a great deal in the Students' Union. His interpersonal and social skills, his numerical competence and scientific background, his confidence and energy, his powers of communication and quick thinking, have all been further developed. To these qualities he has added some experience of organising Union events, a broader understanding of other people and an ability to defend his own point of view. Many a company, particularly in business and commerce, would value these qualities and his energy. It is a great mistake to think that the only benefits of higher education are academic and the piece of paper at the end. And it is a great injustice to stigmatise those who have the courage to change their minds in the first year, and decide to do something different. We need to encourage more people to get some of what higher education has to offer, without using three years' worth of resources.

On the whole, higher education and the students in it are successful. Only 13% drop out; and many of these return when a little older and wiser as part-time students, as mature full-time re-entrants, or via the Open University. Students like Kim and Robin change a great deal. The degree result that Robin gets will depend on the strength of his motivation and the quality of his study methods. If Kim is to perform well in arts, humanities or the social sciences, she will need to develop more confidence and independence of mind. With that proviso, her ability is likely to be the most important factor influencing the class of degree she gets because, whatever subject she takes, she will always try her very best.

Nevertheless, academic success, like many things worthwhile, is often only achieved after a struggle. The struggle not only gives the student some anxiety, but the parents as well, not least because they can't do much about it. Their children are leaving the nest and must fly for themselves. Take comfort. The best academics struggle for excellence too. It's normal.

II.   The use of time
1.   Monitoring the use of time

At university the first three weeks are crucial. It is during that time that students establish their new lifestyle. Changes after that are more difficult. Their new responsibilities are both domestic and academic. They must adjust to the demands of their new residence and the university timetable. They will need to learn to organise their time, to study and learn in new ways, and to make new friends. The rest of this chapter aims to give some tips on these things.

The first thing for students to do is to monitor their use of time. I recommend the following exercise which I have used with hundreds of students. Draw up at least

			Minutes			
0	**10**	**20**	**30**	**40**	**50**	**Hour**
6am						
7am						
8am						
9am						
10am						
11am						
12pm						
1pm						
2pm						
3pm						
4pm						
5pm						
6pm						
7pm						
8pm						
9pm						
10pm						
11pm						
12am						
1am						
2am						

Figure 7.1   Sheet for students to monitor the use of their time.

seven sheets of A4 paper, one for each day of the week, in the manner shown in Figure 7.1. Ten minute blocks of time are marked off between the hours of 6.00am and 3.00am. It assumes that students are asleep between the hours of 3.00am and 6.00am. (That may be an optimistic assumption for some Robins.) At the end of each day, and emphatically no later because otherwise they will forget, the students should place an initial letter indicating the predominant activity in that 10 minute period. (When I give the instructions students often think every 10 minutes is too frequent, but in practice it is a convenient unit. They quickly block off long periods of time, such as for sleep and practical classes, without repeatedly writing S or P. Using longer units results in significant activities, such as journeys on campus, not being represented.)

I have found that the following classification works very well, but there is nothing to stop the students adopting their own if they wish.

L   Lectures and other formal class teaching.

G   Group Discussion, formal seminars, tutorials, group teaching.

P   Practicals, fieldwork, laboratory work organised by teachers.

O   Other academic work, including private studying.

X   Extra-Mural activities, organised recreation, clubs and societies, attendance at church, concerts, theatre, dances, cinema.

I   Informal recreation, having coffee with friends, visiting another's residence, 'chatting with friends', informal discussion.

D   Domestic activities. Getting dressed, having a bath, cooking, eating, cleaning, shopping, any activity essential to life not classified elsewhere.

T   Travel. To and from work, walking between departments, travel for shopping, to and from organised extra-mural activities (X).

S   Sleep, including rest during the day.

M Miscellaneous, including time spent filling in the chart.

You will see that there are 10 items. Apart from "Miscellaneous" they are in three groups: Work, Recreation and Necessities of life. Call them W, R and N, if you like. Of course the amounts of time spent in different kinds of work will vary with the subject of study. Whilst engineers may spend 12 hours a week in Practical work (P), arts students may spend none. Social work and management students may spend a lot of time in Group Discussion (G) and little in Lectures (L). On the other hand the averages for Recreation and Necessities in my researches, shown in Table 7.2, have been remarkably consistent. But they are only averages. Averages hide the variations between individuals. Furthermore averages don't tell us how long students *ought* to spend doing each of these things.

Nonetheless, if a student's lifestyle is very different from other students' he should at least look to see whether he is spending his time wisely. If Robin spends less than 30 hours a week at Work (W), he should write out a list of the tasks he ought to carry out and log them in a written plan of how he is going to spend his time in the coming week. He will say that this particular week was exceptional, but every week is exceptional in higher education. It is important to work steadily, not irregularly, to get the best out of it. If Kim works over 52 hours a week her brain is probably too tired to be efficient. Yet she probably feels that if she works less, she won't get the work done. She may need counselling and her tutor's understanding to have the confidence to rest and relax, before she discovers that she can do as much in less time when she is fresh.

Here is a convenient rule of thumb about the use of private study time (O). For every hour of Lectures students spend nearly the same amount of time looking over their lecture notes - basically learning the facts taught in the lecture (Total = 2L). In maths it would be much more and in arts subjects, less. The preparation time for Group discussions also varies a great deal. A student nominated to give a presentation to the group may spend 10 hours preparing it. Others may do a little recommended reading but spend scarcely a couple of hours. It may average a little over 3 hours for an hour's

W = 37 hours	{ L	8
	{ G	3
	{ P	6
	{ O	20
R = 36 hours	{ X	16
	{ I	20
N = 91 hours	{ D	20
	{ T	10
	{ S	61
	M	3

Table 7.2   Average lengths of time spent by full-time students.

Group discussion (Total = 4G). Although students have to write up their Practical workbooks, compared with the length of the Practicals themselves, the time taken is small; so I shall count it as zero. The remainder of "Other work" time is available to students as "personal thinking time" to read around the subject, to go beyond the tasks set by the teachers, to develop ideas of their own, to explore academic interests, and generally "to develop the powers of the mind" as I discussed in Chapter 2.

Now there is a curious fact. It seems that no matter how much or how little time is spent in Lectures, Group Discussions and Practicals, the average time spent on Work as a whole tends to be the same (around 37 hours). It is Other work time that changes with changes in timetabling. So typically the amount of "personal thinking time" students have is:

37 hours minus (2L plus 4G plus P)hours.

Using the data I have given above that would be:

37 hours minus (16 plus 12 plus 6)hours = 3 hours.

In many subjects the amount that students think on their own has a strong influence on their success. It also leads to a curious conclusion that has been confirmed by experiment: up to a point. If the teachers teach less, students do better because they have time to think more about what they have been taught. 3 hours a week is too little. We tend to teach too much.

There are signs, however, that we are beginning to use more varied teaching methods. It's true that in a recent survey 98% of students experienced lectures, 91% discussions, 82% writing essays and 82% projects and dissertations. But the following increases in the use of other teaching methods over a period of five years were given in the Dearing Report:

Project work by students	61%
Team/group work by students	60%
Use of multimedia	59%
Use of interactive coursework	51%
Use of videos	47%
Team/group teaching by staff	37%
Use of distance learning	24%

III.   Effective reading

Many people say they read slowly when they don't. Nevertheless, students like Kim were unwittingly taught, or taught themselves, to study everything slowly and thoroughly. At university there simply isn't time for that strategy. In most subjects it is more important to know how to gut a text quickly. (There are important exceptions. In quantitative and science subjects, for example, one must follow each step of important calculations or procedures.) Let us imagine Kim, who has to read up on a topic before writing an essay or attending a seminar. Very likely the tutor has recommended a reading list far longer than any human being could manage in the time, because if he only gave a short list, the first students to arrive in the Library would borrow the only copies available and prevent others from reading them until the seminar is over. She should consult the author and subject catalogues in the Library to find out where to go. Very often they are on a computer now.

   When consulting any book on the shelves there are up to four stages she may go through. After any one of those stages she may put the book back on the shelf because she judges that it will no longer merit any further time for her present purpose.

1.   The Pre-View

The first stage is the preview. At this stage she should ask herself 'Is this book of any interest?' and 'How does it relate to the topic of the essay or seminar?'. To answer those questions she should look at the title, the dust jacket and the index. Students often neglect the index, but used intelligently it can direct them to the precise pages required and save a great deal of time.

2.   The Overview

The second stage is the overview. At this stage she should ask, 'How does the author see the subject?', 'What does he include and what issues does he not consider?'. She should already have an indication of the answers to the latter question from having read the dust jacket and contents at the preview stage. But she can get more detail by turning to the Preface, the Conclusion or the Introduction where authors summarise their viewpoint. If the book has more than seven chapters it is useful to try to put them into less than seven groups in order to see the structure of the book and the major questions that the authors have asked themselves when dividing up the subject matter. It is a matter of understanding the way the authors think. Look at the Contents section of this book and try it for yourself. (But if you're really smart you will have noticed how I grouped the chapters at the end of the introductory chapter - Chapter 1.) Many students fail to read the Preface of a book because they think that all the facts are to be found in the chapters. That may be; but it is not the facts that are of first importance, important as they may be, but the ideas that link them together and the most important of those may well be found in the Preface.

   Kim need not read the Preface word by word from beginning to end. She should ignore those sections where the authors thank their secretary (for typing), their partners (for tolerance) and their children (without whose help it would have been written in half the time). She should look for the section that says why they wrote the book. If they are academics it may be a lie – they wrote it to get promotion; but the claimed reason may be that there is a gap in the literature, or that they have a particular viewpoint that has not previously been expressed in print. It is this last point, where the authors declare their bias, that is crucial for the student to absorb. Without that she cannot get an understanding of the book, though she may, like Kim, memorise a lot of the facts contained within it.

3.   The Flip-through

At the third stage, the flip-through, the student will take this process a step further, asking 'What's the gist of what the authors are saying?', 'What's their general argument?', and 'What's worth closer reading?'. To do this she will use the Index and the Contents as before, but she should also develop skipping and skimming techniques. A useful technique when skipping is to read the first sentence in each paragraph in order to get a quick summary. It also helps the student to relate one part of the book or chapter to another because her mind does not become clouded with detail. In skimming, her eye should pass over all the text searching for what seem to be the important concepts. Getting and understanding the concepts commonly used in a discipline is often the most important thing to do when first studying a subject in higher education. Discussing the theories and the facts relevant to them comes later.

4.   Read and Test

The fourth and final stage is to read and test. It is reserved for books, articles or chapters that justify close attention for the student's particular purpose. She should ask herself 'Is what the author says true, good or valid?' and 'What are his sources of evidence or the nature of his reasoning?'. As always in higher education, the student's task is as much to ask questions, to imagine possible answers and to think of ways to test them, as it is to know answers. She should read consciously trying to relate one thing to another. And she should note her personal reactions to what she reads. In particular she should note what she does not understand, rather than recording only what she does.

IV.   Learning from lectures

Lectures are seen as the main method of teaching in higher education. On a recent survey 98% of students received lectures; and that is a paradox. The paradox is this. A lot of research shows that lectures are mostly useful for teaching information, not for developing powerful minds, standards of culture and citizenship, or appropriate emotions, attitudes and motivation. In other words, lectures will not achieve most of the aims we considered important in Chapter 2. They are a legacy from the time when books and other sources of learning were scarce. That explains the paradox - in higher education ways of learning are more important than ways of teaching. That is why the emphasis of this chapter is all about what the students do, not what the teachers do. For Kim and Robin lectures are a new method of learning. Lectures have been described as periods of time during which the notes of the lecturer are transferred to the notebooks of the students without going through the brains of either. Kim and Robin have to learn how to get the best out of them.

What advice can be given? Not a lot. I give some tips in the next section: Review a lecture as soon as possible afterwards. Notice the way the lecturer has organised his subject. Keep trying to cross relate the subject. Note your own thoughts and reactions including what you don't understand. Develop your own shorthand. Identify the crucial issues in discussion and try to relate everything to them. There are some other tips. Lecturers often seem to talk very fast. They don't really, but they sometimes assume that students have fully understood one point when they go on to the next.

The tip is to do a little reading on the topic for half an hour in preparation for the lecture so that understanding is easier. Obviously it is necessary to find out what the next topic will be. I am not saying that the student should study the topic thoroughly before a lecture. That would be difficult and time consuming. It would also leave too little time for follow up study on the last topic. I am saying do a little reading, primarily to grasp the basic concepts and terms in the language of the subject. For this purpose look at elementary textbooks and popular magazines like *"Scientific American"*. These texts will often describe the key issues in a simple manner too. They are usually too elementary for the lecturer to put on his reading list. Reading before a lecture is a matter of doing what comes easily and not feeling guilty about it. Reading after a lecture requires all the intensive skills I describe in section IV.

Concentration in lectures is another problem. It is difficult for everyone. It is easier for those sitting in the middle not too far from the front. In that position the stimulus of the teacher is greater and the lecturer's non-verbal communication is much more easily perceived and interpreted, albeit often unconsciously. Attention soon wanders when the student leans back; all those who are spineless should lean forward. Excessive food, alcohol and warm rooms also make concentration difficult. Athletes and sportsmen work hard at keeping themselves in peak condition. Being an effective student increasingly requires the same dedication, but this is not yet generally recognised.

V.   Note-taking

Many students are anxious about note-taking when they enter higher education, not least mature students who one might have thought would have gained note-taking experience elsewhere. For others note-taking is habitual. Lecturers will tell you that the difference between an undergraduate and a postgraduate is that if you say 'Good morning' to a class of undergraduates they say 'Good morning', whilst postgraduates write it down. As you will see from Table .7.3, there are eight reasons why students might wish to take notes. Some are to help them at the time that they write them. Others are to keep a record for later use.

1.   Aids Concentration

Some students will say, 'I take notes to help me concentrate. It's better than chewing gum'. Particularly on the morning after the night before, lectures of an hour may be a long time to concentrate upon mathematical calculations in economics or physics.

	To help at the time	For a later record
Attention	1. Helps concentration	2. Evidence of attendance
Content	3. Select what's important	4. Syllabus covered
Understand structure	5. See topic development	6. Relate and organise topics
Memory	7. Aids memory	8. Used for revision

Table 7.3   Why take notes?

When, as often happens, the student has one lecture after another, the demands upon concentration are very great. Writing notes keeps the mind active.

2.   Rarely as evidence of attendance

The use of notes to verify that a student has attended a course is now extremely rare in higher education, because even when attendance is obligatory, universities would not check up in that way, even where certificates of attendance are issued.

3.   Select what's important

Many students take notes to select the important points from a lecture, a discussion or a book. When students have done this they may use their knowledge of the important points in several different ways.

4.   Know the syllabus covered

In mathematics and some of the physical sciences students will use their notes as a summary of the syllabus. They may say 'I didn't understand the lecture at the time, but these notes tell me what I have to go and study in the textbooks'.

5.   See the structure of the topic

Other students may say that the important points are like a set of headings showing how a lecturer or an author has developed a description or the steps of an argument. It helps if students know that lectures, articles and books commonly structure their subject matter in one or more of three ways. The most common is to have headings, sub-headings and sub-sub-headings to form a hierarchy. When taking notes in these lectures students need to look out for signals about the lecture structure, such as 'Thirdly', 'Next', 'These may be divided into two types' and so on.

The second is to have a series of steps in a developmental sequence or a chain of reasoning. If students detect this kind of structure, they need not only to identify each of the steps, but to concentrate on the links between one step and the next. Remember a chain of argument is only as strong as its weakest link. Indeed it is interesting that lecturers often cover the blackboard with one equation after another, but they don't write verbal explanations of how one line of a calculation follows from the previous one. They often say it, but they don't write it. The lecturer may say, 'Now if we substitute this expression in that equation, we get . . .'. When attending these lectures it is important to listen for these explanations and note them too. Students have often forgotten them by the time that they get back to their room at night. They can then spend a lot of time and exasperation working them out for themselves. The trouble is that there often isn't time in a lecture to note all these things. The students must overcome this by inventing their own symbols or shorthand for words or explanations that often occur.

The third structure, and the least common, is the problem centred presentation. It is most common in research articles or seminars, because research usually tries to answer a problem. On these occasions the students must constantly ask themselves, 'What is the crux of the problem?' and then try to focus all the facts in a way that is relevant to it. Tutorial discussions may sometimes seem confused because the students have not distinguished the crucial issues. The way to unscramble a confused discussion is to note the crucial questions on different parts of a page, and then note further points under the most appropriate question. When there is only one central question, some people recommend jotting points down connected by lines so that, in the end, the notes look like a tree with a central trunk and many branches and twigs.

6.   Relate and reorganise later study

Other students may see the key points as the framework around which to organise later study. In other words they look for ways to relate additional points, facts, issues, ideas or concepts (call them what you like) to the key points. Particularly when using notes from lectures or a key text in this way, students need to spread them out with a clear layout on broad lined paper so that later ideas, self directed questions and information from other sources can easily be added to the same sheet. Otherwise notes on the same topic will be all over the place on many different sheets. A related and very important use of notes in this way is to take ideas in one section, and deliberately try to relate them to ideas dealt with in other courses or in different parts of the same course. Finding connections between things is a skill important in academic work and most walks of life. To note one's personal thoughts and reactions is an insufficiently used technique to personalise learning, but it is very effective in enhancing memory and thought about a subject. In particular it is important for students to note questions and what they do not understand. Awareness of one's own ignorance guides further study and prevents the wrong choice of exam questions.

7.   Aids memory

Students often fear that by noting one point in a lecture, they will miss another. However there is ample experimental evidence to show that, on balance, taking notes aids students' memories of material presented. This benefit is vastly greater if students re-read their notes the same day as they were written. Furthermore, if this is done, students can usually add points that could not be written at the time.

8.   Revision

Most students use notes as their major source during revision. When students keep reviewing their notes throughout the year, particularly if when doing so, they try to link one part of the syllabus with another, they perform better in examinations. Similarly, those who start revising in earnest six weeks before their exams perform better than those who start only three weeks before. Too often revision is only a process of memorising rather than using information to solve problems or support arguments.

VI. The importance of discussion

Thinking and feeling develop in discussion. That is why discussion is a crucial process in higher education. Universities and colleges exist so that students, including academics, can talk together. Surveys show that after students have left, it is discussion teaching they most remember, most appreciate and from which they learned most. Discussion provides the interaction of minds and the testing of ideas on which research depends. In this sense all students are researchers. They are, or should be, seeking the truth as they see it. Seeking the truth is a process of solving problems. Solving problems should be the focus of written work, reading and discussion.

There are many different kinds of discussion in higher education. There's an encyclopaedia that lists over a hundred. For example, a seminar is a discussion preceded by a presentation of some kind. The presentation may be a student's essay, a talk or a literary text. Some seminars are tutorials. A tutorial is a discussion with a tutor. Tutors typically expect three to five hours preparation for tutorials, if not the submission of written work. What the preparation is will vary with the subject. In science and engineering it may consist of working on, though not necessarily solving, a number of problems. For discussion in the arts, humanities and the social sciences there are seven useful steps in preparation which may occur in the discussion itself:
• clarify terms and concepts,
• decide the major issues,
• concisely state the viewpoints of authors,
• criticise each viewpoint,
• support each viewpoint,
• make up one's own mind, and
• relate the issues to other topics and practical applications.

Taking part in discussions requires a lot of skill. Confidence is necessary to get the full benefit from discussions. Students like Kim will do better if they can contribute early in a discussion. The longer they leave it, the more they feel something must have been said that renders their contribution unintelligent, and the more nervous they become. It is also a good idea to contribute early because early contributions create the framework of the discussion and it is always more difficult to contribute to another person's framework than one's own. Furthermore early contributors don't feel the same pressure to contribute later but, having broken the ice, they usually do.

Kim will get confidence when she realises that criticisms of her ideas are not criticisms of her. Indeed good ideas are those that are most worth testing. When she realises this she will be more willing to comment on other people's ideas. That is when minds begin to be stretched.

The importance of discussions can be illustrated in another way. Robin may skip lectures with impunity, but if he doesn't turn up to tutorials and seminars, questions will soon be asked. If he doesn't turn up when it is his turn to give the initial presentation, or if he turns up having not prepared anything, other students will soon let their feelings be known. (Other students will apply the pressure, not just the tutor; and that may be different from school.) Tutorials and seminars therefore combine strict deadlines with a demand for the highest quality of which the student is capable.

VII.   Personal learning

Personal learning passes unnoticed. When talking of ways of learning in higher education, it is natural to concentrate upon academic learning. If asked, 'What have you learned today?', it is very difficult to say "I've learned some skills of friendship. I can understand better how some other people react to me. I've improved in saying 'No' tactfully. I understand myself better" and so on. Yet these and a million other pieces of interpersonal learning take place in higher education. They don't appear on the syllabus and there are no examinations in them.

You may say, 'Higher education is no different from anywhere else for interpersonal learning.' Yes and no. Residence and university social life create an unusual environment. Sexual relationships are particularly unusual. As one student counsellor put it, "Where else do you sit with your latest partner, opposite your previous partner, every morning at breakfast?". Students are at a time of life when personal relationships are intense, rapidly changing, very public and the subject of discussion by others in a social environment from which there is no escape. Between 6% and 8% of university students drop out for reasons that could be described as social and emotional. These factors affect how long and how hard students can work.

VIII.   Where to get help

Student life can be very stressful. The point should not be over emphasised. The majority of students have the time of their lives as well as working very hard. Nevertheless students (and their lecturers) suffer from more nervous illnesses, even suicides, than otherwise comparable members of the population.

Parents often find it hurtful that students no longer place them in a confidante role. Indeed a parent is often the last person with whom a student would want to discuss personal problems.

Many universities allocate a personal tutor to each student. The system places the tutor in a conflicting relationship - teacher or in loco parentis - and its success depends on the personal chemistry between tutor and student which cannot be guaranteed.

Most universities, and colleges now recognise this and have a number of services to deal with these problems. First there is a student health service. Typically institutions will have one doctor for every two or three thousand students - a better ratio than for the population as a whole. Doctors soon become familiar with the kind of illnesses students present. Very often the doctors will be part-time with students so that they keep their hand in on general medicine during the rest of the week.

Virtually every institution has a counsellor nowadays, though he or she may also double as an academic member of staff. Students usually prefer someone who is wholly independent. Although counselling services are increasingly well used, on the whole students use them too little and too late. They often mistakenly think consultation is a sign of failure, or that the counsellor could not help with their particular concern. At Exeter University I started a Study Counselling service. It was soon used by about 5% of first year students and about half that proportion from later years. These figures suggest that while there are no massive problems about what is expected from students, they should not feel there is something wrong with them when they have difficulties. We all have learning difficulties sometimes.

Many student unions provide a Niteline service. Students seeking help, or simply wanting to talk to someone, can phone at any time of night when other services are not available. Some colleges allocate a second or third year student to act as guide and friend to first years. Unlike relationships with tutors, these friendships can be allowed to wither naturally; but I have known some of them last a lifetime. In many institutions the students' heads of department or the departmental secretaries are sources of informal help. Yet every university will say the same thing: 'If you want help, don't hesitate to ask.' The difficulty for them is not in helping, but in knowing when their help is needed.

IX.   Conclusion

It is not the purpose of this chapter to present a 'how to study guide'. There is a plethora of books for students on that subject. Rather, it attempts to show parents and others how demands placed upon students from their early childhood can influence their later behaviour. In that way it aims to promote understanding. It concentrates on what students have to do - organise their time, read a great deal, learn from lectures and discussions, relate to other people and get help when needed.

The popular view of student life is that it is a time of freedom without responsibility. That is misleading. For most students it is undoubtedly enjoyable, but there are also financial, social and work pressures of a kind not faced by most adults.

Further Reading

Marton Ference, Hounsell Dai and Entwistle Noel (Eds) (1984) The experience of learning. Scottish Academic Press.

Haselgrove Susanne (ed) (1994) The student experience. Open University Press.

8. Assessment of Students

I. There's a fundamental problem when assessing students

All student assessment involves sampling their behaviour. But how can we know that the sample is typical? How can we know that the behaviour assessed gives a valid indication of how they will behave doing other things and in other circumstances? This problem bedevils all assessment. Consider two statements:

> 'People who are good at doing A are generally good at doing B.'
> 'People who are good at doing A are not necessarily good at doing B.'

I am happy to believe both these statements, yet they pull in opposite directions.

To believe that assessments in higher education are valid predictors assumes that the first statement is true. It will be true insofar as A and B are similar. It's a matter of degree. Writing three or four essays in 3 hours is probably more like journalism than marketing, though all three activities involve the arts of communication and persuasion.

If you use the results of assessments, you assume the behaviour assessed is typical for your purpose. If it is not, the assessment is not valid for that purpose. But different people will use assessments for different purposes. So how could assessments in higher education be valid for all of them?

The important point is to recognise that people try to use examinations and other assessments for purposes for which they were not intended. Like any other instrument, assessments are best when they are purpose-designed. Do students themselves know what their assessments are for? In a recent survey, nearly 60% agreed with the statement "What I have to do to get a high grade is clear to me", but 25% said it was not clear. The purposes can be classified into six broad groups.

II. What is assessment for?
1. To assess achievement

For this purpose, the examiner asks the question 'What can the student do?' and compares the answer with the course objectives. Ideally the course objectives will be stated in terms of what the students should be able to do. In practice, that's not possible. Course objectives are rarely very explicit. How can they be? Particularly in non-vocational subjects like history, English and physics, there cannot be a list of precise skills that each participant must achieve. They have to be a bit vague. Each student may legitimately achieve different things within rather vague statements of objectives. Consider, for example, the aims of higher education given in Chapter 2. For this reason, most tests of achievement in higher education try to survey a wide range of knowledge and skills - or at least give students an opportunity to display them.

2.   To predict future behaviour

Although examinations test students on a few selected topics at one particular point in time, they are often used to predict future performance on activities that are quite different. There is little evidence that their predictions are very accurate. For example many examinations consist of writing three or four essays in 3 hours. Most jobs don't. So why should employers think that being good at examinations now, will predict how well a student will do something quite different several years later. Of course many employers don't think that.

There are two points here. One is that people change. They learn. So how do you know that in the future they will behave as they did in the past? The other is the point with which we began. How far does competence at one thing predict competence at another?

3.   To monitor progress

By comparing achievement at different stages of a course, intermittent assessments can be used to monitor students' progress and offer timely advice or support.

4.   To motivate

Intermittent assessments and end of course examinations are powerful motivators. In fact they can be too powerful and create anxiety. Their patterns of anxiety are different. Just before Easter and during the summer term, scarcely a seat can be found in most university libraries as students revise for end of year examinations. For some students, the stress is greater than one might wish so that counselling and student health services are well used during this period. A good tip to deal with examination anxiety is a homeopathic remedy - take some Gelsemium a couple of hours before the examination. It is not addictive and has no side effects.

Intermittent assessment is popularly called "continuous assessment", but it isn't continuous. On the contrary, it creates periodic peaks of anxiety, particularly amongst mature students. For mature students, there is often more at stake. Perhaps they feel higher education is an opportunity that won't come again. Perhaps they sacrificed their job, they are the only wage earner and they feel guilty because they don't spend as much time with their families as they would like. Having an understanding and supportive family is important for all students. That is why students whose parents have experienced higher education often experience less anxiety than 'first generation students'.

5.   To test teaching

It is sometimes assumed that if the examination results are bad, the teaching cannot be much good. That may be so, but the more examination results are said to reflect the performance of the teacher, the less likely they are to reflect the potential of the students. So which do you want to assume? At the level of school work there are often many teachers teaching pupils taking the same GCSEs or O-Levels. So it is possible to compare the performance of one teacher's pupils with those of another. But in higher education, except where several colleges take the same exams, most teachers set their own assessments. So, even though the external examiner from another institution can make comments, judging teachers against a common standard is not possible.

6.   To license to practise

In some subjects, the possession of certificates or degrees is a qualification that entitles the holder to practise in a particular profession. For example, the Government has recently allowed science graduates to teach in schools without teacher training. However professional bodies usually inspect and accredit courses to maintain standards, not to lower them. For example, the Engineering Institutes have imposed increasingly strict requirements upon the syllabus content for degree courses in Engineering. Even so, accreditation cannot guarantee that every graduate will know everything an Engineering Institute might regard as essential. Examinations cannot ask questions on everything, and even if they did, a choice of questions allows students to avoid those subjects on which they feel weakest.

III.   There are problems of validity
1.   Difficulties in test design

An assessment is valid only if it tests the abilities it is intended to test. But it only takes a few moments' thought to realise that it is extremely difficult to design an assessment that will test the aims of higher education. For example, a test of critical thinking should be different from a test of knowledge. Both tests should be different from tests of initiative, creative thinking, responsibility, interpersonal skills, vocational skills, scientific attitudes, hard work, and solving a host of different kinds of problem. This list of skills could be much longer. It might be possible to devise an examination that will test some of them, and test some of them more than others. But, if so, how do you get the right balance between them and how do you decide what the right balance is anyway?

2.   How to train examiners

Let us suppose that the Board of Examiners overcomes all these difficulties when devising an assessment. How, for example,will the Board ensure that each examiner can recognise problem-solving skills and distinguish them from critical thinking?

3.   The marking system

And how will examiners allocate marks for each of these skills? Whatever they decide, the marking system will break down because one candidate will do nothing but display knowledge. Another will show great originality without much knowledge A third may analyse all the possible answers to a question with commendable logic without showing much knowledge or originality, while a fourth may display mature and balanced judgement based more upon intuitive feelings and personal experience. The answers for each of these four candidates may have almost nothing in common. If you allocate 25% of the marks for each of their qualities so that the value of the qualities adds up to 100%, each candidate will fail. You could say that no one person could display all those qualities in the same answer and so it is all right to have the marks allocated for them adding up to well over 100%. In effect, that is what most examiners do, but they don't do it in an additive way. A person who gives twice as many facts will not get twice the number of marks. Students are not judged on quantity, but on the quality of their work. What a student needs to move his mark from 90% to 100% is not more of the same thing that took him from 0% to 10%, but something totally different in quality.

4. Conclusion

In short, the validity of most examinations in higher education is open to question on three counts. First it is difficult to design assessments that test high level intellectual skills. The test setter has to work at an even higher level. Consequently the intellectual and other skills being judged are frequently not specified. Second, most examiners have no training in making these judgements. For example, research has shown that, although examiners talk about the importance of high levels of thinking, most give more marks for factual recall than they would care to admit. Thirdly, there are no generally accepted examining techniques. For example, examiners will happily add marks together or calculate averages as if they were quantities. Examination marks are not numbers. They are qualities. They are based upon judgements of the quality of students' work.

IV. The unreliability of assessments

Most assessments in higher education are open to criticism as being unreliable. That is to say they give inconsistent results. Broadly speaking, there are four kinds of inconsistency.

1. Different examiners

There are inconsistencies between examiners. Some may be generous and some may be strict. Some may award a very narrow range of marks, while others will use the full range from 0 to 100. These inconsistencies can be corrected by simple statistical techniques. These inconsistencies do not matter very much provided examiners place candidates in roughly the same order. But, in general, they don't. They are more likely to do so if they are members of the same department or in some other way have a common background. The external examiner system is supposed to correct this error. He or she is supposed to say whether standards are consistent with those in other institutions. But there is reason to think that the system does not work very well. Sometimes the external examiner is chosen because he is known to a member of the department so that he, too, comes from the same background. Being one visitor amongst many members of the department, he often feels under strong group pressure not to criticise too many things.

2. Inconsistency of a single examiner

There is not only inconsistency between different examiners. Research suggests that the same examiner may give very different marks to the same piece of work on different occasions when he doesn't remember the mark he gave the first time.

3.   Test reliability

Judging from other walks of life, there is also reason to think that some tests give more consistent results than others. For example, objective tests show greater 'test reliability' than essay examinations. The same thing has been found for tests given to school children.

4.   Are standards comparable in different institutions and years?

A more serious problem is the comparability of examinations that purport to assess the same thing. The same subjects may be taught in 100 universities each apparently awarding the same degree, while the curricula and the standards of the examiners may have little in common. Once again we rely upon the external examiner, but even he is unlikely to have experience of more than three institutions in any given year. The idea that he can carry a standard around in his head from one institution to another with unfailing accuracy from year to year is an implicit assumption of the examination system which is frankly ludicrous.

A similar problem applies to maintaining consistent standards from year to year in the same institution in the same subject. A related problem is that even in the same year, few students actually take the same examination when there is a choice of questions. They answer different combinations of questions which are necessarily different with different knowledge and different intellectual skills required. Yet the similarity of the examinations taken is commonly assumed.

5.   Conclusion

The whole examination system at all levels makes massive assumptions about the mental skills required by examinees and the competence of examiners to judge them. There is remarkably little research into the mental processes of either.

V.   Some Factors Related to Examination Performance
1.   Exam technique

Figure 8.1 shows the relationship between certain characteristics of students and their performance in degree examinations. The higher the figure, the closer the relationship. There have been many studies of this kind and the results vary a great deal with the students' subjects.

Nonetheless most of the studies, like this one, show that the strongest relationship to performance in degree examinations is performance in other examinations. One explanation of this is that there are particular examination techniques which help a student to do well but which are not strongly related to anything else. In fact, other research has shown that some students learn the tricks of the trade on how to pass examinations and they use the tricks to good effect. Others know the tricks exist but don't bother to apply them; while a third group who perform least well, don't even realise that these strategies and tactics exist.

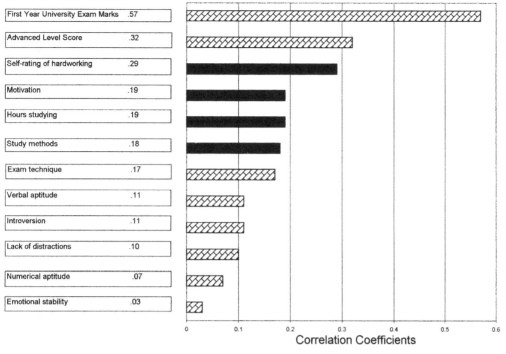

First Year University Exam Marks	.57
Advanced Level Score	.32
Self-rating of hardworking	.29
Motivation	.19
Hours studying	.19
Study methods	.18
Exam technique	.17
Verbal aptitude	.11
Introversion	.11
Lack of distractions	.10
Numerical aptitude	.07
Emotional stability	.03

Correlation Coefficients

Figure 8.1   Correlations with degree results of university students.
Source: N.J.Entwistle, J.Nisbet, D.Entwistle and M.D.Cowell. The academic performance of students I, prediction from scales of motivation and study methods. British Journal of Educational Psychology, Vol. 41 part 3. Nov. 1971.

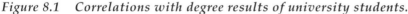

2.   Adjustment to university environments

All this suggests that examination performance is dependent upon a collection of specific skills which are not generalisable to job skills or, indeed, the skills required in doing research. 'He is good at doing examinations so he must be good at doing other things' is, on this evidence, a false assumption. You will notice that the correlation between A Level results and degree performance three years later is much less than the correlation with first year examinations in the same institution. This difference can partly be explained by the time gap being three or more years rather than two. But it seems likely that there is also an environmental factor, some students adjusting to university life better than others. Another factor is that the examiners' approach to assessment will be more consistent within a university department than between that department and an A Level exam board.

However, I must come clean. The closeness of the relationship between A Level scores and degree results varies a lot with what the scores and results were. Look at Figure 8.2. A Level score is quite a good predictor of whether a student will get a 2(i) degree or better. There's a strong relationship between the best scores and getting a

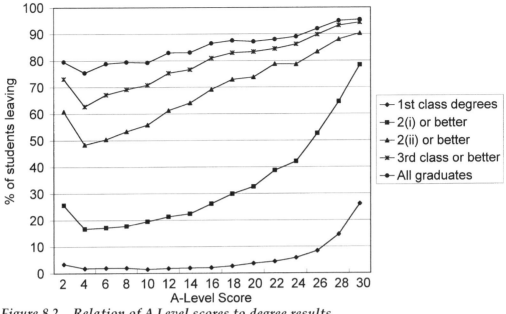

Figure 8.2   Relation of A Level scores to degree results.
Data supplied by Universities Statistical Record

first; but almost no relationship at all when the scores are not so good. The relationships between other degree classes and A Level scores are weak.

3.   Study habits

These environmental factors may well be related to study habits. Those factors with dark shading in Table 8.1 are all related to students' motivation to study. You will see they are more important than intelligence and personality factors. It is known that the amount of study time and its regularity are related to degree performance. So are study skills and the conditions in which students work. For example, in one piece of research it was shown that students who were resident in a tower block at the University of Essex found it uncongenial for private study. They therefore spent less time on their work and performed less well in examinations. As we have seen in Chapter 7, how long students spend in private study depends upon their lifestyle and their pattern of friendships.

4.   Family background

A student's family background is also related to examination performance. In particular, the support of the family is important. If the parents obtained higher education, they pass on helpful attitudes and advice; and the student is less likely to feel that he is out of his social group and has taken a three or four year journey into the unknown.

5.   Social pressures

Social and emotional factors are amongst the most powerful influences upon a student's academic performance. For example when the parents' marriage has been held together by the presence of the child at home, when he or she goes to university, the strains begin to show. Sooner or later the student senses that all is not well and feels a pressure to go home frequently rather than concentrate upon academic work at university.

For most students it is very important to feel that they belong to a group. That group will influence their lifestyle, in particular their working style. Residential life allows relationships to develop intensely and subside with great rapidity. These things disturb the concentration that is essential when studying. Furthermore, research shows that many students are uncertain about their identity. 'Who am I?', 'Where do I fit in?', 'Who else is like me?', 'What am I good at?' and 'What am I going to be?' are all questions that can nag.

6.   Career certainty

Conversely, full-time students who have chosen a career and are working to achieve it, feel more settled. They work with a purpose and perform slightly better than those whose careers are undecided. Not that students should be put under pressure to decide their careers. It is the pressure and anxiety that is harmful.

7.   Academic contacts

Students also do better if they have more contact with academic staff and fewer complaints about the quality of teaching. I don't mean to imply cause and effect. The direction of cause and effect could be the other way round: students who perform badly in examinations may be more reluctant to contact teachers and may wish to justify their poor performance by blaming them.

8.   Personality and social class

The factors I have considered so far are related to the student personality and social class. Students who are more anxious and introverted like Kim are more likely to study hard for long hours than students like Robin who are over-confident and sociable. Similarly, students' fathers who have occupations classified in social classes 1 and 2 are more likely to have received higher education. An important personality factor is related to the students' attitude to authority. It is to do with authoritarian attitudes, dogmatism, fear of uncertainty and ambiguity, and a desire for things to be organised and structured. The effects vary with the student's subject. Students with authoritarian attitudes in higher education, do better in engineering, the physical sciences and law, and will find the arts and social sciences more difficult.

9.   Not intelligence

Finally, you will see from Figure 8.1, that once students are selected for higher education, differences in verbal and numerical abilities are not strongly related to degree performance. Of course a certain level of intelligence is necessary to survive as a student, but differences amongst students are not very great.

VI.   The need to diversify assessment methods

So there's a danger that assessments are unreliable and invalid, not least because a lot of irrelevant factors influence the grades awarded. This danger is greatest when you always use the same assessment method. So there's a need to diversify assessment methods.

Human beings are capable of doing a very wide variety of things that could be judged by other people. Yet in academic examinations, there is an extraordinary concentration upon three hour examinations requiring candidates to write three or four essays.

You might expect that the methods by which students are assessed will vary with the subject they are studying. It is true that science and engineering students are assessed for laboratory and practical work in a way that arts students are not. Yet this is an extreme case. On the whole students in different disciplines are assessed in similar ways. Table 8.3 shows the percentage of students assessed by various methods. But it doesn't show how much of each method students have to face. Although diversity is increasing, there remains a great need to devise methods of assessment that will test the full range of skills we require from our graduates.

Let us look at some of the factors that could be varied.

1.   Terminal or intermittent assessment?

Typically essay examinations occur at the end of the course. These contrast with intermittent assessments which occur periodically throughout the course.

2.   Fixed length or more open-ended assessments?

Essay examinations are usually a fixed length of time. Course work, projects, dissertations and theses are more open-ended, though they, too, must usually be submitted by a certain date and have a limited number of words. They are therefore less intensive. It's a bit like the difference between the 3000 metres steeplechase and seeing how far you can run in a given period of time. Intermittent assessments with their periodic hurdles are more like the steeplechase. Different people are best suited to different events and the training required is quite different for each.

3.   Measure the time taken to do a task

Within the period specified for most assessments in higher education, the tasks themselves are untimed. The examiner doesn't know, and probably doesn't care, whether a candidate took half an hour or an hour and a half to answer a given question. This is unlike a secretary taking a shorthand test where both the quality of what she does, and how long she takes to do it, are factors assessed. The neglect of 'time taken' in higher education is curious because, in most aspects of human performance, it is a very sensitive measure. For example, two candidates could solve a mathematical problem but one might see the way to do it straight away while another

	Medicine	Sciences	Social Studies	Humanities	All
Essays	91	83	96	97	87
Written examinations	85	98	90	97	86
Projects/dissertations	86	90	79	71	81
Oral presentations	71	74	74	73	73
Other course work	44	50	37	32	46
Practical write-ups	55	97	31	8	39
Multiple choice questions	49	47	33	22	31
Work-based learning	39	16	19	10	22

Table 8.3.   Types of assessment used on courses.
Source: Dearing Report 1997

might hesitate a long time. The proliferation of computer terminals makes information on how long a candidate takes to answer a question much more readily available to examiners than in the past. But, so far as we know, no-one has experimented with this factor.

Another variable is the number of attempts to achieve a goal. In the driving test and most Open University exams, it doesn't matter how many attempts you make so long as you pass in the end. But if you fail, most universities limit the number of 're-sits' you can have.

4.   Maximum power or minimum standard?
Most academic examinations are "maximum power" assessments. They ask the question 'How good is this candidate?'. But university and professional entrance examinations ask the question 'Has a "minimum standard" been reached?'.

5.   Pass–fail, grades or profiles?
Minimum standard assessments are usually of a pass-fail type while a range of grades are more commonly awarded in tests of maximum power. A third option which is becoming increasingly popular is for the examiner to write descriptive profiles of each candidate's performance. These are called "assessment profiles". They are not only most useful to employers, but they give constructive feedback to candidates. In some cases, this permits them to work at their weak points. The desire to rank people in order of merit is a conceptual mistake. Different people have different qualities and should be valued for what they are. Jones may be better than Smith at one task, whilst on another, their merit is the other way round. It would be unfair to say that one of them is a better person than the other. It depends what you are talking about. The temptation to put people along a single line should be resisted.

6.   Impressionistic, analytical or objective marking?
There are three different ways of judging examination performance. In "impression marking" the examiner gives a number or a letter grade according to his subjective impression of the student's work. In "analytical marking" a certain number of marks

may be awarded for each item on a checklist of criteria. How far a candidate has satisfied a criterion can still be a little subjective. In objective tests, (such as the multiple choice 'tick in a box' type used in some medical schools), the marking and grading is sufficiently objective that it can be done by computer.

7.   The type of skills assessed
Examinations vary not only in their subject matter but in whether the skills tested are cognitive (to do with knowledge and thinking), affective (to do with attitudes, motivation and feelings) or motor (including manual and other physical skills). Owing to the historical dominance of university examinations over the whole educational system, educational assessments have concentrated almost entirely upon cognitive skills. Other aspects of human beings have been grossly neglected. The growth of profile assessments will enable examiners to value the variety of qualities different students have. In particular the introduction of profile assessments could place more value upon attitudes, personality and motor skills.

8.   All tasks compulsory or offer a choice?
Because all assessments are a sampling process, examinations are highly selective in what they assess. They are made even more selective when candidates are offered a choice of questions. Understandably, candidates prefer to have a choice, but examinations are less valid and reliable when they do.

VII.   Implications
1.   The skills taught and tested are too narrow
We've seen earlier that traditional examinations require a restricted range of skills. The skills required to write three or four essays in 3 hours in geography are much the same as those required to do the same thing when the subject is history, English, or sociology. That's why students who do well in one examination tend to be the students who do well in others, but they don't necessarily do so well when the skills required are something different. That's why I said the skills required in higher education ought to be more wide ranging. We need to widen the skills we teach. That process has begun with an increase in the number of courses that include vocational experience.

2.   Broaden the criteria for selecting students
Most students who reach higher education have already acquired many of the skills required for writing 3 hour essay examinations. My worry is that the system eliminates a lot of people who are not good examinees, who not only merit higher education, but who could contribute much more to us all if they had it. We don't know the size of that problem. We do know that there are a lot of people who drop out of the education rat race who later return and do quite well.

3.   Play the examination game to win
Until the skills required are broadened, the best way to get a start in life is to concentrate on the narrow range of skills required at present. In short, it pays to play

the system. The best way to learn examination skills is to practise doing exams. It's a very obvious point, but it is very rare for students to sit down and work with that level of intensity for three hours. Imagine training an athlete to compete in the 1500 metres. Surely you would get him to run 1500 metres at some stage if not quite frequently? It's not like that in education, perhaps because we half recognise that doing examinations is not what we really want our students to be able to do. We don't really believe in the system we're operating. It's just that we can't think of a feasible alternative. That's precisely what I think we've got to do, and there are new technologies now that should make alternatives more feasible.

VIII. Conclusion

If you've read this chapter and you have a social conscience, you should feel a little uneasy about how we decide who are the 'best' students, and how others are rejected. Perhaps our assessment systems should search for that which is good in every man and woman - an open-minded search, not a predetermined test with fixed criteria. After all, an open-minded search is very consistent with the values of higher education.

Further Reading

John Heywood, (1987) Assessment in Higher Education. Wiley.

9.   Projects and Research

Research is a process of seeking the truth. At the end of Chapter 3 I said, "the search for, and the proclamation of, the truth as one sees it are the fundamental activities of higher education." "To seek the truth is fundamental to freedom. To apply it is fundamental to progress." So research should be a process common to all higher education, indeed all education in a free society. We should all be researchers now.

I.   We should all be researchers now

Hitherto, in school education, and too often at higher education, there has been an emphasis upon the teacher presenting knowledge for pupils and students to remember and regurgitate on the examination paper, but there are signs that this is changing. The General Certificate of Secondary Education (GCSE) in England and Wales, combined with increasing vocational activities in school education throughout Britain, is increasing the amount of project work carried out by pupils in schools.

These developments affect higher education. Instead of recruiting students who have successfully passed A Level examinations, there is an increasing number of students who have undertaken projects, either at school or at work, using techniques similar to those employed in research. Undergraduate courses will no longer be a proving ground from which students will then go on to do research at postgraduate level. There will be more of a research attitude amongst undergraduates. This is all for the good. The major adjustment required will be by the academic staffs in higher education, not by their students.

In the early 1990s the Government tried to create closer links with employers. Under the Enterprise in Higher Education scheme (EHE), institutions were offered up to a million pounds over five years if all their students obtained work experience as part of their courses, and employers were involved in their assessment. In practice this meant that the students carried out projects. From the employers' point of view, except when deputising during holidays, temporary student labour is more disruptive than helpful. But many had a small self-contained project, or enquiry that had never been done and was eminently suitable for students, and which could be jointly assessed by employer and university as the EHE required. Although the offer has now closed, the increase in project work at undergraduate level remains.

Incidentally, the scheme arose from the common belief that most students have no work experience. That's not true; not a lot, maybe; but educationally a little experience is very different from none at all. Even if we ignore all part-time students, those on sandwich courses and all continuing education students, and confine our attention only to full-timers, nearly half have been employed before they enter higher education. Furthermore, according to the Government's loans survey, 59% obtain vacation employment for an average of 8 weeks per year - more than EHE offered over three or four years.

If parents and employers have never done any research, and most will not, they may have the same non-comprehension about what goes on in higher education as parents have had in the past 25 years about what goes on in primary schools. This chapter gives an understanding of some of the skills, frustrations and procedures involved.

Of course, the procedures for carrying out projects and research will vary enormously from one subject to another. I can only make sweeping generalisations here.

II.   Twelve typical stages in research
1.   Deciding the general area
Typically, the procedures will follow 12 stages. First of all, in the humanities students will need to decide the general area they would like to research. Straight away, there is here a difference from most undergraduate studies. Students probably negotiate their topics with their likely tutors. The tutors are not setting topics that the students must study. Very likely students will choose tutors to suit their interests.

At this stage, the students' ideas about what they want to investigate may be very vague and broad. In science and engineering it is much more common for a possible supervisor to recommend specific topics, problems or areas for investigation in the light of industrial needs or research in progress in their department.

In the case of an aspiring postgraduate research student, at this stage the potential supervisor is also probably weighing up whether to accept the student. The teacher has to decide whether the candidate is appropriately qualified, whether the necessary resources (such as library, computing, laboratory facilities and technical assistance) will be available, whether, if from overseas, the student's English is good enough, whether the student has the self-motivation to complete the research in a reasonable amount of time, and whether the supervision of this student doing this piece of research is in his/ her list of priorities.

Once they have been taken on, students and their supervisors should discuss how they will work together and how often they should meet. Students have the responsibility to raise any difficulties however small, to say what kind of advice they find most helpful and to give an annual report on their progress for the head of department. Supervisors have the responsibility to set standards, maintain regular contact, to monitor progress, to provide opportunities for instruction in research methods, and at postgraduate level to arrange seminars to which their students will make a contribution.

2.   An inventory of resources
At the second stage, the tutor is likely to send the student away to find out what the available resources are for investigating topics in his broad area of interest. In the past, students have often confined this search to the library. I suspect that with growing practical and occupational experience, combined with the Internet and other sources of information, the student has many more resources from which to choose.

If the student is writing a thesis, the university or departmental Library will probably have copies of theses done by previous students. It is a good idea for students to look at some of these at this early stage. It helps to set standards and to give some idea of what to aim for. To leave this until later sometimes results in narrowing the student's vision of what might be done and how it might be presented.

Throughout all the stages of doing a project, it is advisable for students to keep a rough notebook in which they jot down any ideas, however half formed or foolish they may seem. This notebook is purely personal. It is quite a good idea to date each jotting so that students can monitor their development of ideas. It can be quite encouraging for students to realise how they have progressed. It is also quite a good idea to initial those ideas that are the student's own. It is vital to keep a record of all bibliographic sources that have been consulted. Once lost, trying to find out the detail of references previously consulted can be extremely frustrating and time-consuming later on.

It's quite a good idea to write on the right-hand page only and to reserve the left-hand page for later comment. Sometimes the left-hand page develops into a conversation with oneself about the pros and cons of a particular idea or procedure. Writing objections, counter-arguments and their rejoinders helps to clarify thoughts. It thereby advances the maturity and subtlety of what is eventually written. You might think it is easier to use a wordprocessor than a notebook; but it isn't. Noteworthy ideas come at most inconvenient times. You can't carry a computer everywhere you go.

3.   Narrowing the field

Whether or not students have access to an abundance of resources, the tutors will encourage them to narrow down their area of interest to something minute and manageable. Students always choose topics that are too big because they don't realise how much there is to know. When first being ignorant of a subject, they don't realise how big it is. The sooner students can narrow down their topics of investigation, the less time they need take to study topics they will later discard as irrelevant to their investigation.

4.   Specifying the precise research problem

The fourth stage is to decide the theme or problem that the student wants to justify, criticise or solve. It's a good idea to express it in the form of a question. Answering that question then becomes the focus of everything the researcher does. There are four criteria of a good research question.
- It must be clearly, simply and precisely stated.
- It must be limited in scope.
- Its assumptions should be consistent with most, but not necessarily all, known facts.
- It should be answerable both in principle and in practice.

If, instead of a question, you talk about a problem to be solved or a hypothesis to be tested or verified, the language may be slightly different, but essentially these four criteria are the same.

The practical limitations include the time required for the project, the student's budget, his/her ability and ensuring the necessary co-operation of other people, such as the general public in a social survey or lab technicians in chemistry. A very important fifth characteristic is required for postgraduate research degrees, particularly PhDs – the degree is only awarded for original work, so the problem must allow originality.

In practice, the question, theme or problem nearly always has to be progressively refined and modified to make it more precise and consistent with the known facts. Its progressive refinement continues to take place during the next four stages.

Specifying the problem is a crucial stage in any research. The research can't begin until it is clear. Indeed some universities will not accept a student's registration for a research degree until it is clear what the student wants to investigate. Most university faculty boards are the same.

5.   Getting the topic and oneself organised

The fifth stage is to plan the organisation of the project. Students needs to plan their time and to outline the possible argument that their project or thesis will present. Of course it is only tentative at this stage but each step of an argument has to be justified and so the steps show what has to be investigated to make each justification possible.

Wise students will make sure that they let their supervisor see their organisation at this stage. The organisation is crucial to showing how the argument or "thesis" is developed. Supervisors and their students should have agreed at stage 1 how often they should meet to discuss progress, but we believe that from stage 4 or 5 it should be once a week, though not necessarily for very long.

6.   Labelling rough notes

Having decided how the eventual presentation is likely to be organised, the student will probably see it as having several chapters or sections. The sixth stage is to go through all notes and rough jottings and mark them with a number or some other indication of the section(s) where the ideas might be used. Very many may not be used at all and can be put on one side. Don't throw them away irretrievably because, as plans change, there are always one or two you'll want to refer to.

This review often sparks other ideas which should also be noted. It is also useful to insert cross-references as they come to mind.

7.   Planning observation

Another consequence of deciding the organisation and likely plan of the project is that the students can decide much more easily what is relevant and what is irrelevant. They can read and study selectively. Whilst reading selectively, they should continue to jot down ideas and thoughts in the rough notebook. In particular, they should consider what fieldwork, experiments or other investigations need to be carried out to justify the answer to their research question. This stage includes designing experiments, questionnaires and other instruments for observations. It includes working out what could be inferred from all possible observations in advance of making them. This avoids going to a lot of trouble to conduct experiments or make other observations and then discovering that they couldn't possibly prove anything anyway. These activities need to be prepared and their detail incorporated into the plan outlined at stage 5.

Consultation with the tutor is particularly important at this stage. It very often happens that the discussion sends one back to stage 4 to redefine the research question and go through to stage 7 again. That should not be regarded as a retrograde step. On the contrary, refining the research question and removing errors of thinking, is progress.

8.   Observation

The eighth stage is to carry out the fieldwork, laboratory work or other form of investigation. Again, it is necessary to jot down observations at the time because they won't be remembered later. This is particularly important where students have to report on their own methods and procedures. Many thoughts and observations occur during practical work which cannot be recalled later. So these too need to be captured at the time and recorded in the student's notebook. Quite often, these thoughts lead the students to modify their arguments, their diagnosis of the problem or their suggested solution to it. Indeed, this is the purpose of a pilot investigation. Consequently, it is also not unusual for the students to return to stage 4 again from stage 8. In some forms of postgraduate research, this cycle is repeated many times. For example, in literary research, a student may revise his interpretation and argument after observation of new sources.

9.   Planning the presentation of work done

Stage 9 is to plan the presentation of the project. Of course this will vary enormously with the subject. In art and architecture, it may consist of a display with almost no written material at all. In computing, it might consist of programmes or files on disk. In some other subjects, it may consist of little more than the results of a calculation. What I shall present here is typical of the requirements for many of the social sciences. What is required in arts subjects on the one hand, and the physical sciences on the other is different in degree rather than of a totally different kind.

First, the student needs to set the research question or theme in its context. The student needs to present a review of the literature as part of this context, not as a separate exercise presented before the real issues are considered. The bibliography will need to be built up as references are made. The context will include the background of the subject, an explanation of why this project was undertaken and not another one, its theoretical and/or its practical implications, and possible hypotheses, themes or arguments that could be explored. Next, the aim of the project needs to be set out in a way that is precise, objective, non-emotive, non-judgemental, and factual. The student should use concise, short and reasoned sentences.

When describing the method of investigation, the acid test is "Could the investigation be replicated from this description?" So quite a bit of detail needs to be included in this section and some of it, (e.g. sample questionnaires) may be included in an appendix. It should always be remembered that constructive criticism is the fundamental process of higher education. So students need to justify what they have done and anticipate objections. In particular, they need to explain why they used experimental methods, questionnaires, interviews, direct observations, participative research, or whatever methods were used. They need to explain the design of their investigation. For example, if they are comparing one thing with another, what controls are observed to ensure that the comparison is a fair one? They need to explain and justify the criteria and/or the measuring instruments used. For example, can they be justified as convenient or because they have previously been used by other researchers? They need to consider whether other criteria are relevant or possible.

Most projects and investigations involve sampling. In many projects, they will need to justify the size of the sample, whether it is typical and how they obtained it.

The principle of replication requires that procedures should be succinctly explained in a matter-of-fact style. Where equipment has been used (e.g. in the physical sciences) it should be described. Where instructions or questions have been devised (e.g. in the social sciences) these should be specified.

Almost no matter what the project, students gather a mass of information and data. Their problem is how to present the findings or results clearly. What information can be put in diagrams? What can be tabulated? Very often the presentation of results reveals that certain unexplored and unexpected relationships should be investigated. These further investigations should be restricted to those that are relevant and, in practice, are often restricted by the time available. Yet it is remarkable how often students present sets of data without ever considering how they might be related. Another very common error in the presentation of results is to give an interpretation of them. It is important to stick to the facts objectively at this stage and to distinguish data from its interpretation. Interpretation is presented after the results and is always more subjective and controversial.

The interpretation of data and its relationships are commonly considered in a "Discussion" section. Part of students' critical skill lies in the questions they ask themselves. How is the data related to research reviewed at the beginning? How does it fit existing theories and, most of all, how can it be applied to the problem, hypothesis, or argument? What are the limitations of the data? What factors influenced the results and what reservations do the students have when making their interpretations? What objections might other people make to their interpretations? What points might they concede to their opponents and what and how will they rebut those criticisms they reject? If conversations have not been recorded in the ideas notebook, the students are left to do a lot of important thinking all at once. Inevitably important points are omitted. If the points have been recorded, this stage is a matter of selecting and organising the arguments recorded.

The conclusion should summarise the findings of the project in terms of the aims presented at the beginning and giving the crucial evidence that supports or defeats those aims.

Finally, students should write an abstract which summarises the structure and sequence of their project. This abstract will be placed at the beginning, after the title page but before the contents page.

10.   Preparing the physical appearance of the presentation

Many examining authorities have quite strict regulations about how theses and other projects should be presented. For example they may say that there should be three copies typed with double spacing on a certain size of paper bound in a certain way with gold lettering of a specific size on the outside and a specified form of words on the title page inside. Ideally students should look at these regulations at stages 2 or 5. Stage 10 is the very latest.

The thing to avoid is to start writing up or preparing illustrations without having a clear conception of the physical appearance of the work. Similarly it is important to prepare illustrations, maps, tables, photographs or any other visual material before "writing up". Not only can a picture save a thousand words, but if the illustrations are not done first, they tend not to illustrate the text because the text is not written with reference to them.

It is a common error to start writing up too soon. It feels good to get a chapter or two out of the way early, but it usually results in arguments not hanging together, because the students have started to write before they have seen how all their facts interconnect. To write rough notes early is a good idea; to attempt the final version early is folly. This error is all the more tempting now that wordprocessors give the illusion that modifications can easily be made later. Details can; but it is very difficult to change the whole tone of an argument once one's mind has committed itself to seeing the subject in one (less mature) way.

11.   Writing up

Several points need to be made about the style of the "Write-up" itself. Firstly, it should be consistent. So there should be a consistent hierarchy, numbering and style of headings. The same applies to tables, graphs and other illustrations, as well as to footnotes and appendices. There are two or three accepted ways of setting out bibliographical references. Whatever style is chosen, the student should be consistent.

As I have suggested, the language should be crisp and simple, but that is not always easy because, by their nature, the topics are often quite complex. For this reason, students have to teach the technical terms of their subject to their readers as they goes along. The same applies to abbreviations and acronyms.

Another major difficulty is what to include and what to leave out. It is usually best to leave out jokes, anecdotes and personal whims. It is also usually best to include some self-criticisms and reservations about one's conclusions. What is not so clear is whether to include influential abortions and digressions. By "abortions", I mean those parts of the project the student undertook which came to nothing. Many projects and research involve exploring avenues which turn out to be cul-de-sacs. They turn out to be a waste of time, yet the student may have learned something from them which influenced the way the project was subsequently developed. In this case, it seems right to include something about the exploration that was abandoned. Influential abortions have to be mentioned. The same applies to digressions. Exclude irrelevant digressions, but include those that are necessary as briefly as reasonably possible.

Above all, students should remember that they are writing an argument. They have been seeking the truth by a process of criticism and now they must seek to persuade their readers of what they have found. The steps of the argument can be made clearer by the use of quintessential headings which, when read in sequence, summarise the argument. Another trick is to imagine that what they write is always being contested by a hostile critic. By anticipating and answering all the objections to their arguments, their theses will be made all the stronger. Another tip to make the argument clearer is to provide "tracking devices". That is to say, they should refer to other parts of their project so that the reader can follow the argument as a whole. The most important "tracking device" is the abstract or summary that should appear at the beginning. This should be written last so that it reflects the structure and sequence of the project as a whole.

As an examiner, I don't read a thesis like a novel. I jump around. I often ask myself, "What did the candidate actually do?" So I look at the methodology and the research instruments (e.g. questionnaires) quite early, to see whether the conclusions could possibly have been drawn from what the student did. So the "tracking devices" such as the Abstract and the detail of the Contents page, are important to me.

12.   Take a holiday, review, amend and present

When the first full draft of a thesis or project is complete, parents and friends may need to persuade the student to take a break from it. Every author knows the problem of being so close and bound up in one's subject that one cannot see it from the point of view of the reader. That's the time to take a holiday. Students will see what they have written in a different light, and see it as a whole, when they return after a fortnight. That is the time to make amendments. Even the abstract can be written then. After that, with the supervisor's consent, it can go to the binders and then to assessment.

At this time the student often experiences contradictory feelings. Parents and friends may need to appreciate them. On the one hand there is great relief that it is finished; on the other, anxiety and tension about a viva examination or what the assessor will think of it.

III.   The lonely life of the postgraduate research student

Section II gives a general account of what a student has to do regardless of whether he or she is doing an undergraduate project or postgraduate research. But postgraduate research is bigger in scope, takes longer, is more thorough, demands originality, and often results in a different lifestyle.

It is the difference in lifestyle that sometimes takes a student by surprise and leaves parents at home not understanding what has changed. Let us imagine that Robin (from Chapter 7) goes away to university, enjoys himself, gets on very well in his department, does well in his final exams and, because of his lively, open-minded argumentative style, is invited to stay on to do research. When he begins his research his friends have left. He no longer has a regular diet of lectures and seminars. He sees his tutor briefly only once a week. The social life of the university is beginning to get repetitive. He feels unsure of himself in unexplored academic territory. Within his department he feels in a 'no man's land'. He is no longer an undergraduate and can feel uncomfortable mixing with them because he teaches some of them either in seminars or supervising in the laboratory. Yet he is not a member of academic staff either.

All this adds up to being lonely. His parents at home realise that his attitude has changed, but they are in no position to know what is different. Don't get me wrong: most postgraduates thoroughly enjoy their work and often find that the release from the routine of lectures and exams is a breath of fresh air. Nonetheless the experience of loneliness has happened sufficiently often to warrant a mention.

The role of the supervisor is crucial. According to one study, most postgraduates prefer their supervisor to be knowledgeable, available for consultation, helpful, stimulating and critical in that order of importance. When asked about the difficulties they encountered students mentioned isolation, their inadequate knowledge of research methods and the need to limit the size of their project. Part-timers mentioned the lack of time.

You may wonder why some of the cleverest young people in the land wish to spend up to five of the best years of their lives investigating an apparently remote and esoteric problem. There are two reasons. First they do it out of interest, personal advancement, self-fulfilment and because they enjoyed their first degree. Secondly, the problems are not usually remote and esoteric when their implications are understood.

Research students normally write a thesis which they must discuss and defend against the criticisms of two or three examiners, the third of whom might be their own supervisor. This sounds pretty daunting, but most examiners are kindly without relaxing the standards they treasure.

Although there has been a fuss about the number of PhD students who don't complete their degree successfully, 84% are successful in science and engineering subjects (coincidentally the same figure as for undergraduates in those subjects). Only 67% are successful in the humanities, but as very few of them are supported by taxpayers' money, the fuss is less justified. See Figure 9.3.

IV.   Who does what research and why?

Virtually every academic in universities can do research. Not everyone chooses to do so particularly in the 1992 universities which have no long research tradition. In other higher education colleges timetables and funding don't make it easy.

1.   Undergraduates

We've already seen in Chapter 7 that project methods are increasing on undergraduate courses. They may not always involve the discovery of new knowledge (research) or new interpretations of old knowledge (scholarship), but the trend is clear.

2.   Postgraduates

Again, postgraduate degrees don't necessarily involve research. There are plenty of "taught masters" courses, but the *number* of postgraduate students jumping from bachelors' degrees to doctoral research (PhDs or DPhils) without taking a Masters degree first, either by research or traditional examination, has been erratically increasing for 30 years.

Students who get a first, or upper second, class degree are often unofficially regarded as qualified to do research. This is odd because there are studies showing that the best researchers, such as Fellows of the Royal Society, can be hard working plodders, like Kim in Chapter 7, who originally got a lower second or worse. Timed examinations favour quick thinkers like Robin.

Nonetheless, if we look at the *percentage* of students getting an upper second or better who go on to do PhD research, (what is called the PhD Qualified Participation Rate) we find first, that it has erratically decreased, and secondly, that there are marked differences between disciplines. (See Table 9.1.) If you want a PhD, study chemistry! In fact 40% of all PhDs are in science, 17% in Engineering, and 8% in medicine; whilst there are 14%, 7% and 7% in social science, languages and other arts respectively.

There are also marked differences between science and humanities, as shown in Table 9.2.

In recent years students have been put under pressure to complete their PhDs in three years in the mistaken belief that those who take longer don't complete successfully. As Figure 9.3 shows, PhD students who take over 5 years are less likely to get the degree; but even after 8 or more years, the majority are still successful.

3.   Academic staff

In Chapter 12 we shall see that research by academic staff is funded from two major sources – what is often called "the dual funding system". Roughly half university expenditure is on research, 20% being an element within the Higher Education Funding Councils' (HEFCs) grants for the work of tenured staff; and 30% from the research councils, Government departments, industry, charities and other organisations sponsoring specific research and services.

The trouble with the HEFCs paying every tenured academic to do research is that some are more productive than others. Not surprisingly the HEFCs decided to carry out a Research Assessment Exercise (RAE, see Chapter 11) in order to reward those who are judged to be more productive.

This has certain consequences. The roles of teacher and researcher have become more separate because good researchers, allowed to concentrate on research, do less teaching. Others choose not to compete for research recognition and get better funding by taking more students. There has also been a great increase in temporary Research Assistants in units such as those listed in Table 9.4, because they can be employed more cheaply than tenured academics. Furthermore, academic staff themselves are increasingly on short term contracts. This is changing the whole process and structure of university employment.

4.   What research?

To establish areas of excellence there is more institutional control of research. It is more often done in teams and specialist research centres are set up. Successful research centres may then attract long term funding from the research councils. Table 9.4 shows the size of the research councils' budgets, what they currently sponsor and which

	Full-Time	Part-Time
Chemistry	50	5
Physics	28	3
Maths	17	3
Business Management	11	10
Psychology	7	5
Geography	7	2
English	7	2
History	3	2
Law	1	0

Table 9.1   Typical PhD Qualified Participation Rates for selected subjects

	Science	Humanities
The average time taken to complete a PhD	5.2 years	6.0 years
The proportion who complete their PhD successfully	84%	67%
The proportion who enrol as part-time	18%	37%

Table 9.2   Science and Humanities PhD students compared.

universities are so favoured. It will be seen that Oxford, Cambridge, Edinburgh and the specialist colleges of London dominate.

What's missing? The research councils are wholly science or social science based. The arts and humanities are not listed. They seem like the poor relations of university research. The Dearing Committee recommended that an Arts and Humanities Research Council should be established and the Government has now done so.

5.   Why do research?

Cynically, you might say academics do research to get promotion. And you'd be right. Whatever the protestations of Vice Chancellors that teaching and research count equally, in practice academic promotion is more on the basis of research than teaching.

That said, what are the functions of research? Why should money be spent on it? There are three main groups of functions.

(a) First there are functions concerned with the development of science, new ideas, scientific standards, the bases upon which new fields of knowledge grow and can be quickly applied (e.g. the application of transistors in the 1970s) and the inter-linking of academic disciplines.

Money for these functions comes from three main sources: the research councils in the form of research contracts with academic institutions; the HEFCs as part of the 20% dual funding mentioned above; and other grant making bodies including Government Departments.

(b) A second group of functions is concerned more with applied research and development than with fundamental discoveries. Their immediate effects are economic and social, rather than a permanent contribution to a body of knowledge. The contracts are mostly with industry and government. They are policy driven. They include

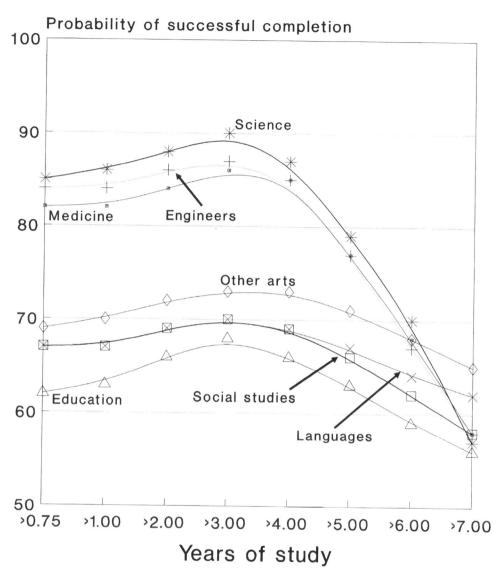

Figure 9.3   The probability of PhD success having taken n years.
Higher Education Statistics Agency data. Note the contrasts between the sciences and humanities

contributions to government enquiries; strategic research; applications of new ideas to industry; and checking the feasibility of plans, proposals and policies.

(c) A third group consists of contributions to the educational and cultural life of the nation. The money comes mostly from local authorities in the form of student grants and from individuals in the form of their fees. These functions include advancing knowledge; creating an enquiring attitude of mind in the community; fostering

Biotechnology and Biological Sciences Research Council (BBSRC) £183.30

Arable Crop	Bristol	Genomes	Edinburgh
Food	Reading	Molecular Sciences	Oxford
Grassland and Environment	Aberystwyth	Neuroscience	Sussex
Biochemical Engineering	UC London		

Council for the Central Laboratory of the Research Councils (CCLRC)   £1.45m

Economic and Social Research Council (ESRC) £64.89m

History of Population and Social Structure		African Economies	Oxford
	Cambridge	Globalisation and Regionalisation	Warwick
Business	Cambridge	Science, Technology, Energy and Environment	
Economic Learning and Social Evolution		Policy	Sussex
	UC London	Complex Product System Innovation	
Economic Performance	LSE		Sussex
Urban Studies	Glasgow.	Financial Markets	LSE
Fiscal Studies	London	Human Communication	Edinburgh
International Employment Relations		Micro-Social Change	Essex
	Warwick	Transport	UC London
Organisations and Innovation	Sheffield	Business Process Resource	Warwick
Development, Instruction and Training		Applied Social Surveys	City Univ.
	Nottingham	Economic Policy	LSE
Ethnic Relations	Warwick	Economic and Social Data Archive	Essex
Elections and Social Trends	City	International Bibliography of	
Social Integration and Exclusion	LSE	Social the Sciences	LSE
Innovation and Competition	UMIST	Qualitative Data Archival Resource	Essex
Social and Economic Global Environment		Access to Data in Europe	Durham
	East Anglia		

Table 9.4   Topics supported by the Research Councils in University Research Units 1998.
UC = University College; LSE = London School of Economics. Table continued opposite.

national, community and individual awareness; and producing future generations of
scientists, teachers and other professions.

Since the 1980s there has been a growing emphasis on (b). However, because (b)
depends upon (a), in the long run that emphasis will be self defeating if a balance is not
maintained.

V.   Conclusion

My conclusion is both optimistic and pessimistic. The greater use of projects with a
research element in schools and at undergraduate level suggests a widening of research
skills in the community. That is an important democratic antidote to the growing
power of a few people to control what and how information is available. On the other
hand governmental and financial controls may in practice restrict knowledge and
freedom. It is to that we must now turn.

Further Reading

Whiston Thomas G. and Geiger Roger L. (Eds) (1992) Research and Higher Education. Society for
Research into Higher Education and Open University Press

Medical Research Council (MRC) £289.07m

Neuropharmacology	Oxford	Human Movement and	Inst Neurology
Neuropathogenesis	Edinburgh	Balance	London
Biochemical and Clinical		Immunochemistry	Oxford
Magnetic Resonance-	Oxford	Environment and Health	Leicester
Biostatistics	Cambridge	Hearing	Nottingham
Brain Metabolism	Edinburgh	Molecular Medicine	Oxford
Cancer Trials	Cambridge	Inter-disciplinary Cognitive Neuroscience	
Cell Mutation	Sussex		Oxford
Immunology	Oxford	Cell Biology	UC London
Brain Repair	Cambridge	Medical Sociology	Glasgow
Human Toxicity	Leicester	Molecular Haematology	Oxford
Molecular Sciences	Oxford	Molecular Immunopathology	
Protein Engineering	Cambridge		Cambridge
Child Psychiatry	London	Muscle and Cell Motility	Kings London
Cognitive Development	London	Neurochemical Pathology	Newcastle
Cyclotron	Hammersmith Lond	Protein Phosphorylation	Dundee
Epidemiology	Barts London	Reproductive Biology	Edinburgh
Biochemical Genetics	UC London	Social, Genetic and	
Human Genetics	Edinburgh	Developmental Psychiatry	London
Human Genome Mapping	Cambridge	Toxicology	Leicester
		Virology	Glasgow

Engineering and Physical Science Research Council (EPSRC) £386.37m

Process Systems Engineering	Imperial	Material for High	Birmingham &
Semiconductor Materials	Imperial London	Performance Applications	Swansea
Biomedical Materials	Royal Free Hospital	Superconductivity	Cambridge
	London	Optoelectronics	Southampton
Polymers	Bradford, Leeds	Surfaces	Manchester &
	and Durham		Liverpool

Scottish Agricultural and Biological Research Institutes

Biomaths and Stats Scotland	Edinburgh	Land Use	Aberdeen

Natural Environment Research Council (NERC) £165.11m

Antarctic Survey	Cambridge	Population Biology	Imperial Lond
Oceanography	Southampton	Atmospheric Chemistry	Cambridge
Sea Mammals	St Andrews	Mesoscale Meteorology	Reading
Aquatic Biochemistry	Stirling	Global Atmospheric Modelling	Reading
Comparative Plant Ecology	Sheffield	Environmental Systems	Reading

Particle Physics and Astronomy Research Council (PPARC) £191.85

Astronomy	Hawaii

*Table 9.4 (Cont)   Topics supported by the Research Councils in University Research
Units 1998.*

UC = University College; LSE = London School of Economics

10. What Academic Freedom is, Why it Matters

Most members of the public understand the freedom of the press and they know why it is important. But they don't understand what academic freedom is, nor why it matters. It seems as if academics are claiming a freedom for themselves, a special privilege. Ordinary people resent others seeming to claim special privileges. The freedom of the press is seen as important for everyone. Academic freedom is not seen in the same way. But it ought to be. Both are about freedom of information - freedom to know the truth.

In one way academic freedom is even more precious. It is not a freedom for big business, for newspaper tycoons or television sponsors. It is a freedom for individuals from which everyone benefits. Yet it does involve claiming a special right and that claim needs to be justified. The arguments are not easy; so you may find they need a lot of thought.

According to Professor John Searle, there are two complementary arguments, one based upon a group of general civil liberties, the other upon the special nature of academic work. Both arguments are required to justify academic freedom as a special right.

I.   The General and Special Arguments
1.   The General Argument
According to the General Argument, any citizen in a democratic country is free (1) to seek the truth about anything he likes and (2) to pass it on to others, unless these two freedoms are explicitly taken away. They are taken away in the case of military secrets, recent Cabinet papers, one company's chemical formulae, another company's production processes, certain aspects of personal privacy and so on. For most employees these freedoms are also surrendered during working hours, because it is implicit in their contracts that their time will be spent on the employer's business, not seeking and proclaiming the truth. But of course, in the special case of higher education, that is the employer's business. It is a lecturer's job to seek and proclaim the truth as he sees it, not as others see it. It would therefore be contrary to the implicit contract between employer and employee to take those two freedoms away, to sack, or penalise in some other way, a lecturer who exercised either of them.

2.   The Special Argument
According to the Special Argument, academics claim a special authority and privilege not possessed by the general population as a civil right. It is therefore applicable in countries that don't have the same civil liberties as Britain. Even in this country there are government regulations controlling the selection and rejection of the disabled and other minority groups for employment, the contents of packaged food, the statements made in advertisements, and the certification of building standards.

But in the pursuit of their profession academic staff claim freedom from government controls on the selection and rejection of students, the content of curricula, the need for students to consider their opinions, and the validation and issue of certificates on the competence of others.

Universities, and colleges are largely government funded (which most employers, food producers, advertisers and builders are not), but the institutions claim considerable immunity from government controls. He who pays the piper does not entirely call the tune. This special immunity needs special justification.

The crux of the Special Argument is:

(a) a claim that academics have a special competence or expertise in the search for truth, and

(b) a claim that academics possess a special knowledge of their subject.

This distinction is important. Ultimately to deny (a) is to suppress the truth. To deny (b) is to challenge the intellectual authority of academics. Nonetheless (a) and (b) overlap in that, if academics carry out research, they can claim knowledge not possessed by others, because they have explored and tested ideas at the frontiers of knowledge not visited by others.

II.   Some Assumptions

These arguments make a number of assumptions.

1.   Functions

Both arguments depend upon the assumption that the functions of institutions of higher education include seeking and disseminating the truth.

2.   Contracts

They also assume an implicit contract between an academic and his institution that allows the academic certain freedoms. In particular, on the Special Argument, unlike most employees' contracts, the implied contract doesn't necessarily bind the academic to do what the employer wants. The contract isn't, and cannot be, to prejudge, find and proclaim particular assertions to be true. It is to seek, find and proclaim the truth irrespective of what the institution might think about it. Thus an academic should not be penalized for finding and publishing unpopular truths.

3.   Free critical enquiry

Both arguments make a set of assumptions about how knowledge is obtained. As we saw in Chapter 3, since the time of Descartes, the accepted methods for obtaining knowledge have not been to refer to the dogma of presupposed authorities, but have included independent observation, the principle of public verification, the replication of experiment, and the dissemination, testing and contesting of opinions. This process of critical enquiry, in which no belief is immune from doubt, has become fundamental to the pursuit of knowledge in higher education.

4.   Civil liberties

Fourthly, whatever the exceptions, the General Argument assumes certain civil liberties as the norm in our society, in particular, the rights to discover and disseminate the truth unhindered.

5.   Consequentialist and non-consequentialist values of knowledge

There could be two different assumptions about the value of academic freedom based upon its consequences. In our kind of society it is easier than in some others to value the truth, not only as sometimes useful, but as having some intrinsic and possibly absolute value. For example, academics such as F. R. Leavis claimed to study a subject "for its own sake", not for its beneficial application or other consequences. In societies without our civil liberties, academic freedom would have to be given as a special privilege. It would probably, though not necessarily, be given because the knowledge consequent upon such freedom was seen as useful or beneficial.

III.   Distinguishing various freedoms that are claimed

The philosophy of academic freedom is remarkably tangled. To untangle it, I have tried to distinguish two arguments and five assumptions. The term "academic freedom" sometimes means different things. So now I must separate out the different freedoms being claimed.

A   Freedom of enquiry - freedom to pursue the truth unhindered, and by methods of doubt, criticism, discussion and testing of any belief.
B   Freedom to disseminate the truth as one sees it.
C   Freedom to express doubts and criticisms of any belief.
D   Freedom to decide who shall be members of one's own academic institution(s). Freedom to decide the content of academic courses.
F   Freedom to decide upon the competence and certification of others.
G   Freedom to teach in private and without inspection. Freedom to teach by whatever method one chooses.

Freedom to do these things is taken to mean that academics who do them will be free from threats, particularly threats of dismissal. A is particularly to do with research. E to H are mostly to do with teaching. B, C and D are related to both.

IV.   Which of these claims are justified?

Freedoms A, B and C may be justified on the grounds of general civil liberties (the General Argument) combined with a claim that academics have a special competence to search for the truth. (That is (a) in the Special Argument.) And because of that competence, there is a claim to have authority in the subject researched. (That is (a) combined with (b)).

D, E and F are not based upon the need for free critical enquiry, but upon institutional autonomy and a claim by academics to have authority because they know more than other people about their subject. That is (b) in the Special Argument. But that doesn't seem to me to be a good enough reason to justify a unique freedom for academics.

I think that freedoms claimed solely on the basis of special knowledge (that is claim (b)) look shaky when analysed in detail, particularly when one begins to define the area of special knowledge. So I think academic freedom is about A, B and C, not D to H. Any application of the Special Argument to matters of teaching needs to take account of how far the same arguments apply to schoolteachers. For example, schoolteachers might claim

Freedoms E and F on the grounds that they have knowledge of their subject at the level at which they teach it.

The academics' case for special freedoms in teaching would look stronger if their teaching was always near the frontiers of his research. But obviously it often isn't. Not only do academics not always teach near the frontiers, they are bound to teach subjects that are not at all close to their area of research. The counter claim that research activity assists, rather than competes with, teaching proficiency, also lacks objective supporting evidence.

Claim (b) seems weak when applied to teaching. This is particularly relevant to E, because professional bodies, for example those in engineering and law, are increasingly saying what degree courses must include for professional recognition.

I accept that academics should be free to teach subjects of their choice, but little follows from that. If an academic is free to teach astrology, that is no reason why the institution should validate the course or why students should attend. In other words the academic may be free to proclaim the truth as he sees it, but there is no obligation on anyone else either to listen or to think that his opinion is worthwhile.

Furthermore, it also does not follow that, because academics are free to disseminate the truth as they see it in subjects of their choice, they should not be compelled to teach the truth as they see it in subjects not of their choice. Freedom B may imply freedom from disseminating ideas one believes to be false, and Freedoms B and C imply a freedom to express one's belief that certain truths are unimportant; but however much these arguments justify the inclusion of X in the syllabus, additional arguments are required to justify the exclusion of Y. Admittedly, additional arguments may not be hard to find. For example, 'if staff are free to teach X, time, staff or other resources may not be available to teach Y. If the authorities insist they teach Y, they will not be free to teach X.' The important point, however, is that the onus is then upon academics to show what the circumstances are and that the principles of academic freedom apply.

I can't see that either G or H can be justified on the basis of academic freedom. Indeed the duty to disseminate the truth might lead us to open our classes more widely, rather than claim a right to privacy. If academics want to claim such freedoms, I think they must find other arguments pretty quickly. The demands for greater accountability and quality controls are now broadly accepted.

Similarly, I cannot see that academics are protected from redundancy on grounds of academic freedom. They may be protected by their contracts, the laws on unfair dismissal, or some other reason. But that is another matter. Again, Freedoms D, E and F might be better argued on the basis of institutional autonomy combined with special knowledge (that is Special Argument (b)) rather than on the basis of academic freedom.

It must sound from all this that I am attacking the notion of academic freedom itself. I am not. I am saying that academic freedom is an important value and has important moral principles associated with it. Such freedoms constantly need to be defended, not least at the present time. To do so we should be clear what those freedoms are and how they are justified. There is a danger that important freedoms will be discredited if they are confused with untenable claims. In the long run such freedoms are defended by favourable public opinion and the responsibility with which they are used. Academic freedom is a right, but it is also a privilege that is earned.

I conclude that "academic freedom" is a general name for several freedoms mostly to do with research (rather like "democracy" is a general name for several different freedoms). Yet, in practice, university teachers who do no research, usually have greater security of tenure than researchers who do no teaching.

V.   Why does academic freedom matter?

It is essential to the preservation of democracy. That is why I said at the beginning of this chapter that academic freedom is important for everyone, not just academics.

The first thing any undemocratic government does is to try to control the minds of its people. In a democracy, there is a sense in which, ultimately, the minds of the people control the government. Nowadays the first thing any revolution or counter revolution tries to do is to control the radio and television stations. It is they, more than the newspapers, that have most immediate control over the information available to the people.

How can the people decide what is true, what is biased opinion, and what is propaganda? They need two things: the best possible methods and resources for finding out; and independent voices so that the findings are impartially interpreted and expressed.

Academics provide both these things when they have the freedom to do so. The best possible methods are research methods, and academics have the necessary expertise. Independence necessitates freedom from pressures and vested interests. Academics speak out with independent minds when they have the necessary freedom.

That is why their freedom is important. That is why academics and universities are often the first to suffer at the hands of repressive governments and why universities are often the first sources of protest.

We should be clear that it is not only governments that wish to control information or to present facts in a particular light. Commercial interests may wish to do the same. For example, it was not in the interests of the tobacco industry to research the effects of smoking upon health. Their advertisements and sponsorships deliberately associated smoking with healthy activities like sport. Nor was it in the short term interests of successive governments. Governments obtained substantial revenues from tobacco taxes.

It was university research that showed the effects and the broadcasting media that publicised them. History is now repeating itself with the effects of alcohol. Its harm has been known for centuries, but only by its harm being thoroughly demonstrated can the political power of the brewing lobby be defeated. As with smoking, millions will suffer and die until the truth is fully known. These are only two examples. The marketing and persuasion industries are now big business.

A higher education system dependent upon commerce and industry will not seek or proclaim the truth, because it will not be financed to find the truths that commerce and industry do not want to face, do not want others to know, and do not see as having value to them. Fundamental research, which may at first sight appear to have no obvious application, will be neglected. Laser technology and microwave ovens would not exist if academics had not been funded to explore freely, ideas that industry thought were useless. Furthermore, the 50 year failure of the tobacco industry to publish its research into the harmful effects of smoking, shows the importance of independent research and the freedom to publish the truth as one sees it.

During the 1980s it was Government policy to increase the dependence of higher education upon commerce and industry. To that extent there was a loss of freedom. The Government itself used its power to influence what information was available to the public. The BBC was pressured not to show certain programmes so that its Director General resigned. The author of "Spycatcher" was pursued vindictively in the international courts. Research funds diminished and there were moves to reduce the number of university departments doing research. Not least in the field of education itself, research was virtually restricted to topics related to the Government's own policies. Then its publication was restricted when the findings did not support those policies (e.g. research into the 'popularity' of school boards and parent power).

The Conservative Government also tried to prevent the following amendment to the Education Reform Act passing into law: the University "Commissioners shall have regard to the need to ensure that academic staff have freedom within the law to question and test received wisdom, and to put forward new ideas and controversial or unpopular opinions, without placing themselves in jeopardy of losing their jobs or privileges they may have at their institutions". The Government failed. The reader should ask, 'Why did it try; and why did it fail?'

Against this, many previous governments have worked to preserve academic freedom and other democratic rights. Governments have supported the rights and practices of their oppositions because they recognise that the processes of democracy are not only of greater value than their own policies, but belong to a higher order of values. The difference is like the difference between 'statesmanship' and 'political skill'.

Academic freedom to pursue and proclaim the truth as one sees it, is a higher order value of this kind. To say that where governments pay for research, governments should control what is researched and what is published, is to fail to understand this point. Industries may commission research for their exclusive use. Government sponsorship of research, unlike commercial and industrial sponsorship, should not be in its own interests, but on behalf of its people; and it has an obligation to let the people know its findings. That is a different kind of responsibility.

The crucial conclusion is that academics need to be financed by governments to seek and proclaim the truth wherever it leads them, because that should be part of governments' policies to preserve and enhance democracy. This requires that governments trust academics and that academics earn that trust. Both have obligations towards the other. There's nothing wrong in mutual trust; no family, or any other relationship, can survive without it. Mutual trust is strengthened when it is constantly tested and constantly passes the test. In this respect academic freedom is no different from any other freedom.

Further Reading

Malcolm Tight (Ed) (1988) Academic Freedom and Responsibility. Open University Press, Society for Research into Higher Education.

Russell, Conrad (1993) Academic Freedom. Routledge.

11. Pressures for Accountability

The last chapter gave a strong endorsement for the concept of academic freedom, but it would be unrealistic in the present day to leave the subject without recognising the pressures under which that concept operates. In terms of the current jargon there has to be a balance between institutional autonomy and public accountability. On the one hand higher education institutions are corporate entities with freedom to conduct their own business. On the other hand there are so many vested interests in the products of higher education that there are in practice limitations on the way in which they are able to conduct their affairs. This chapter will therefore look at the reasons for that pressure, the way in which it manifests itself and some of the institutional consequences.

It is always tempting to talk in terms of recent changes in higher education, in particular the consequences of reduced funding. These are often seen as beginning with the return of the Conservative Government in 1979 and the 1981 cuts in university grants (see chapter 3). There is a temptation to hark back to a golden age of institutional and academic freedom in which there were no encumbrances to academic activity. Undoubtedly the pace of change has quickened in the 1980s and 1990s. But in reality the universities have been dependent upon government funding and therefore vulnerable to government pressure ever since the rapid expansion of the 1960s (see chapter 3). The Robbins Report furthered that expansion, the availability of free tuition and local authority grants for full-time undergraduate students. This dependence was in some respects hidden for the decade or so after the Robbins Report because higher education and the economy were in an expansionary phase; but during the 1980s and 1990s three things happened to focus pressure on institutional accountability:
- reduction in public expenditure as an arm of government policy,
- development of higher education from an elite system to a mass system and
- a shift in emphasis away from seeing higher education as an end in itself primarily for the benefit of the individual, towards being an output for the benefit of society in general and the economy in particular.

Given these developments it is tempting to see the growth in demands for accountability as accompanying financial constraint. Whilst that is partially so, the fact is that the voice of stakeholders in higher education has increasingly become louder.

I.   Who are these stakeholders and how have they affected higher education?

The simple answer to the first part of the question is that we are all in some way stakeholders. We all have a stake in living in a civilized society. Such societies are typified by the search for knowledge and the education of each generation. That is what higher education is all about. Such matters were considered in the last chapter, but at a more mundane level most of us pay taxes which go towards paying for the system of higher education.

More specific interests accompany this general interest. For instance:

- the government represents the public when choosing how best to spend public funds;
- staff want to harmonise their personal aspirations with the furtherance of the well-being of the institution in which they work;
- students expect higher education to further their career aspirations;
- employers expect a certain level of attainment from graduates and a way of thinking which often transcends the specific subject of study;
- local communities increasingly see the economic advantages of having a higher education institution within their locality;
- many professional bodies accept qualifications from higher education institutions as meeting in whole or in part their membership requirements;
- research councils invest in the innovation associated with higher education;
- commercial bodies contract for services and expect institutions to deliver the service consistent with their contractual obligations;
- donors and benefactors expect their interests to be honoured.

The list could go on, but the point is that there are many interests to which higher education institutions have to be accountable. We shall look in a little more detail at three examples to show how the interests of stakeholders impinge on the autonomy of institutions.

First there is the general public which wants value for the money which is spent on their behalf in maintaining a system of higher education . Many members of the general public may not be qualified to judge whether institutions of higher education are providing good value but national mechanisms have been established to provide reports on the quality of the research and teaching being undertaken in universities. We shall have more to say about this later, but as the number of students has increased so has the Government's financial commitment, and the demand for proof of value for money. In the days when a few universities were operating an elite system it was possible to manage, some would say get away with, a self-regulated system of peer review with external examiners and occasional visitations from the University Grants Committee and professional bodies. Effective as that system might have been, in an expanded system justice not only has to be done but seen to be done.

Second, and almost inextricably linked to the first point, is the government's desire to have some measure by which to allocate increasingly scarce resources. Elsewhere in this book (Chapter 12) the methods of funding higher education is explained in more detail, but by emphasising the accountability function, government, through the funding councils, has developed a mechanism for rewarding institutions according to the perceived quality of their output. This has been particularly so in the case of the funding of research which has been increasingly selective.

Third, as higher education has increasingly been viewed in terms of meeting the economic needs of the nation, so there has been pressure on institutions to be accountable for providing courses which fit students for future employment. This trend has not only raised the voice of employers in the context of higher education provision, it has coincided with a period when students have been expected to meet a higher cost of their education with a shift from grants to loans and the payment of tuition fees. As a consequence the design of degree courses has been subject to external pressure and in many institutions has become modular in form allowing students a wider choice of subjects, providing the arts student with an opportunity to become computer literate or the science student to study a language. The importance of transferable skills has a higher profile now than formerly.

II.   How has the demand for greater accountability been met in practice?

During the 1980s and 1990s the response to the demand for greater accountability has been seen at three levels: national, institutional and individual. We shall look briefly at each in turn.

1.   At a national level

At a national level, research and teaching performance of each institution are now monitored. In 1986 the first Research Assessment Exercise (RAE) was undertaken by the then University Grants Committee and has been followed by similar exercises at three or four yearly intervals. The object of the exercise is two fold: to grade each department's research on the basis of the output of its staff over the previous assessment period; and secondly to allocate resources on the basis of those assessments - the higher the assessment the more money is allocated by the funding council. For each exercise, specialist panels are established by the funding councils. For the RAE 1996 exercise there were 69 panels covering the various subjects to be assessed. Institutions can choose which members of staff to submit for assessment. The way in which funding is allocated is by multiplying the quality grading by the quantity of staff submitted. By limiting the number of staff it submits to those who are "research active" an institution can aim for a higher quality but lower volume calculation. The institution submits a wide range of data for assessment. These data for the RAE 2001 will include the publication record of the staff it has submitted; numbers of research students and other personnel supervised; research degrees awarded; 'esteem indicators' such as prizes, medals or other awards; conference and media presentations; details of research grants and a statement of its research plans together with any other information which it thinks might be to its advantage. The panels, which do not visit the institutions, review the documentation and grade departments on a seven point scale ranging from 1 to 5*. (For historical reasons point 3 is divided into 3a and 3b and point 5 is divided into 5 and 5*.) As examples of what each grade represents, a grade 1 rating would indicate "research quality that equates to attainable levels of national excellence in none, or virtually none, of the sub-areas of activity". A grade 3a would indicate "research quality that equates to attainable levels of national excellence in virtually all sub-areas of activity, or to international level in some and to national level in others comprising a majority". A grade 5* would indicate "research quality that equates to attainable levels of international excellence in a majority of sub-areas of activity and attainable levels of national excellence in all others". As an indication of the volume of work involved, for the 1996 RAE a total of 2,896 submissions were received from 192 higher education institutions which listed 55,893 active researchers.

Assessment of research was followed in the early 1990s by a system of Teaching Quality Assessment (TQA) with panels of assessors from the funding councils undertaking periodic visits to departments. Those assessors are experts in the subject except for the chairman of the panel who would be trained on the assessment process itself. Departments submit self-assessments stating their aims and objectives and giving a critical analysis of their strengths and weaknesses. The assessment panel then visit the department over a four day period. Meetings with staff and students are held; classes are observed and a wide range of documentation reviewed. That documentation includes information given to students about their courses, student intake and progression data, description of arrangements for student support, internal quality assurance arrangements and examples of students' work. At the end of the visit the panel grades the department according to six core aspects of provision. Those core aspects are

- curriculum design, content and organisation;
- teaching, learning and assessment;
- student progression and achievement;
- student support and guidance;
- learning resources;
- quality assurance and enhancement.

There is a four point grading scale applied to each of the six core aspects. Grade 1 is an unsatisfactory grade where the aims and/or objectives as set by the department are not met. Grades 2 to 4 represent various levels of satisfactory provision. If at least one of the core aspects is graded 1 a second assessment visit takes place within a year. A second unsatisfactory report would be likely to lead to the funding council removing money from the university's annual grant for that subject. Public reports are issued on the basis of the visits and are available from the funding councils. This is an important potential source of information for applicants, parents, employers, students and other academics.

In addition to the assessment of teaching and research by the funding councils, a Higher Education Quality Council was established by universities themselves in 1992 to conduct audits to ensure that quality assurance procedures were in place and operational within each institution. Unlike the TQA visits, these do not look at subject provision, but concern themselves with whether the institutions have internal mechanisms in place for ensuring the quality of provision. Concern over the burden of documentation and work for the two external quality assurance systems led to the establishment in 1997 of a single quality assurance body, the Quality Assurance Agency (QAA), which will bring together institutional and subject reviews.

2.   At an institutional level

At an institutional level there has been a need to react to these national initiatives. In addition to long established practices, there has developed a more systematic form of quality assurance. It is likely, for instance, that:

- there will be regular reviews of departmental performance, often involving senior and well respected figures from other institutions;
- degree curricula will be subject to formal review at periodic intervals to ensure that they are meeting current demand;
- a senior member of staff will be responsible for quality assurance issues (and in each department too);
- quality issues will be recognised in the formal committee structure of the institution by the establishment of a Quality Assurance Committee which will have a responsibility for monitoring procedures and practices at a departmental, faculty and institutional level;
- departmental activities, particularly in the field of research, are likely to be more focused than previously, partly because of financial restrictions, but also to ensure quality of output.

3.   At an individual level

At an individual level these national and institutional developments have placed more pressure on members of staff. Although the concept of academic freedom may in principle give them wide discretion in what to teach and the areas of their research, in practice they are likely to find that their time is managed and geared towards achieving the quality ratings which will attract funds or give their department a high reputation in those criteria judged by external monitoring bodies. Whilst there may still be room for the lone humanities researcher utilising library facilities, the chances are that the scientific researcher will need to be part of a team to use limited resources to best advantage. In addition to managed activities, members of staff will also be subject to annual appraisal schemes during which they will discuss with their head of department their objectives for the following year and the extent to which they have met their objectives over the previous twelve months. What is discussed is usually confidential, but to a point, academics' targets have to be known by their immediate colleagues, and in many institutions it is accepted that the superior may use a record of the appraisal process when reporting to the Promotions Committee.

How are researchers appraised?

Mostly by their publications. The quality of research is judged by fellow academics, journal editors and publishers' advisers before it is published; and it is then reviewed, criticised or cited afterwards. It is assumed that these judges use criteria appropriate to the subject, such as whether the findings will stand the test of time, whether the methods are original and could be replicated, whether interpretations of the facts are reasonable, whether it will stimulate new work and so on. So the amount published and, more rarely, the number of citations, have been used as indicators of the quality of an academic's research.

Such data is available, but it has its limitations. If promotion were dependent on the number of articles published, academics might be tempted to publish many short superficial articles in less reputable journals. Promotion decisions often involve comparing lecturers in different departments, but cross discipline comparisons can be very misleading. Journal space varies with the subject. So do conventions of co-authorship. If a Chemistry PhD student publishes work it is common practice to attach the supervisor's name as co-author. In arts subjects that would be very unusual. Furthermore, a reasonable publication rate will vary with the nature of the work. A scholarly article in philosophy or literature may take years to work out and write; whilst an article reporting some experimental research could take only two or three months from conception to completion. ("Scholarship" involves the reinterpretation of information already known; whilst "research" involves a procedure to discover new information.)

Citation data is necessarily delayed. Authors of highly original work may not be quoted very much because it is difficult to understand or not in the mainstream of current work. Again, there are subject differences. Citation is used more in the humanities than in the physical sciences partly because the latter are more quantitative, less dependent on context for their interpretation and less controversial.

One way over these difficulties when judging who is a good academic, is to consult others in the same field. This is known as "peer review". Peers, it is said, will be able to make a subjective judgement on the quality of research and scholarship published, taking all the variables into account. The big question with peer review is to decide who the peers should be. If only a few are consulted their preferences, not to say their prejudices, would be very influential. Peers in other institutions are often rivals for funding. The unfair influence of individuals can be offset by consulting a large number of peers, but that is expensive and time consuming.

More recently measures based on the amount of research funding obtained have been used; but this too, is not a very fair indicator of who is doing a good job. Funding is subject to the whims of fashion and current policies of grant awarding bodies. Research topics, even within the same subject, vary greatly in expense. Peer review by the Research Councils (which sponsor research) could be influenced by an inner circle of researchers each scratching each other's back. There have also been frequent complaints that, owing to Government pressure, those engaged in fundamental research have been penalised compared with those whose research is more applied.

How can the quality of teaching be judged?

By using many indicators. Most promotion committees use too few. Pre-1992 universities don't evaluate teaching enough; but a variety of indicators have long been used in Public Sector Higher Education (PSHE) by Her Majesty's Inspectors and, at the time of course validation and review, by the Council for National Academic Awards.

Indicators can be classified under four groups of questions: 'What are the consequences of the teaching?', 'What opinions are there about it?', 'How can the teacher's techniques be described?', and 'What resources are used?'.

The consequences include the quality of students' work in assignments, presentations and examinations, and their attendance at classes. It is possible to observe how students develop on a course or to compare their development with those on other courses either at the time or later.

Opinions may be sought from students, the teachers' colleagues, staff development officers, inspectors and the teachers themselves by questionnaires or interviews. Each of these groups get their opinions in different ways. There are other indicators of opinions, for example the number of students who choose to take a teacher's optional course or who withdraw from it. Some form of opinion collection is by far the most common technique. The observations on which the opinions are based and the techniques of collecting them vary a great deal (e.g. how far interviews are structured or the design of questionnaires.) A very great deal of research on students' opinions of teaching shows they are very consistent in the opinions they hold, but it remains doubtful how far the opinions are valid when compared with more objective observations.

Techniques to describe what teacher do are always selective. They include observing teaching, or video-recording it for later analysis, analysing critical incidents in the classroom, conducting case studies, keeping diaries, looking at the teachers' records of their teaching and an analysis of workloads.

An inventory of the resources used by a teacher cannot, on its own, be used to judge the quality of teaching; but it can help to build up a picture. Copies of reading lists, instructions for student assignments, handouts, and a record of visual aids and other equipment used in teaching can all give an indication of a teacher's style.

The first serious attempts to find ways to evaluate teaching were concerned with the individual teachers, their improvement and promotion. They assumed that the quality of teaching is reflected in the amount students learn and the behaviour of the teacher. Psychologists study learning and behaviour. Accordingly the methods of psychologists are prominent in those I have just described.

Conclusion

All these quality assurance procedures are aimed at satisfying the various stakeholders in higher education that their interests, whether they be financial or otherwise, are being met. Given the diversity of interests and the wide ranging responsibilities of higher education institutions perhaps it is inevitable that such mechanisms should be in place. The balance that has to be struck is to ensure that such mechanisms do not themselves create such bureaucratic procedures as to stifle academic ingenuity and divert institutions and their staff from the fulfilment of their academic potential.

Further Reading

Johnes, Jill and Taylor, Jim (1990) Performance indicators in Higher Education. Society for Research into Higher Education.

12. The Government and Finance of Institutions

I.   The general character of academic management

Some people may see institutions of higher education as run by a Prime Ministerial figure called a Vice Chancellor, Director or Principal who is chosen by a "sovereign" who is either the Chancellor of a University or the Chairman of the Governing Body. Other people may think of universities as elite institutions governed by an elite of the elite, namely a group of senior professors who discuss, persuade and cajole in the corridors of power. Non-academic staff may see their institution as being run by the academics. Junior academic staff may feel dominated by departmental pressures, particularly the whims of their head of department. Heads of department will see themselves as trying to accommodate all the wishes of individuals in their department within institutional policies, financial constraints and student numbers laid down 'from outside' or 'from above'. Students may think they are governed by an impersonal set of rules and unwritten precedents followed by a group of equally faceless administrators who always seem to be acting at the behest of an inscrutable committee.

Although each of these perceptions may have a small element of truth, each impression is a travesty of academic government. The way decisions are taken in academic government is far more subtle and complex. No doubt this is why people talk about "academic politics". The process is political in the sense that there is management and manipulation of power. Rules are made or changed and there are sanctions that can be applied to ensure that they are observed. These rules are the result of discussions in which conflicting interests and perspectives will be expressed. Furthermore, academic institutions have explicit policies which they try to pursue. At best these will be consistent with the individual aims and objectives of their members, but there may well be tension between institutional and individual aspirations. Counterparts could be found for each of these features in national government, but so they could in a factory or almost any other organisation.

There are other respects in which academic politics are quite different from national politics. For one thing there are no political parties. Membership of an institution is more temporary than membership of a nation. This leads to a different pattern of membership and a commitment that is more intense, but shorter. Academics choose their institution, while very few of us choose the nation to which we belong.

Furthermore, and this is important, in most academic institutions there is not a simple line management forming a hierarchy of power. Most lecturers have several interests and obligations - they may teach on several courses and be involved in more than one research project, each having a different leader. Lecturers largely manage their own time and prioritise their own work, although in recent years financial pressures and the link between research output and funding have led to a more managed approach to the setting of departmental, and hence individual, priorities. In many respects, however, procedures of line management drawn from the world of industry sit uncomfortably in an academic setting. As Charles Handy has pointed out, academic institutions are managed by consent, not consensus. Management needs to check that what they propose is acceptable. Individuals want to be consulted rather than participate in management. Authority is not imposed from above, but by consent from below. Academics see themselves as a resource. They want the right to disagree based upon reciprocal respect and trust. Academic institutions are not like industry. Academics are judged by their peers, not least by those in the same field in other institutions. That would be extraordinary in textile or motor manufacture. In a factory many people work together to produce relatively few products. Individuals on the assembly line may have little idea how their work contributes to the whole. Their co-ordination is therefore an essential feature of management. In the academic world the same degree of co-ordination is not intrinsic to the methods of production. While individuals may work together to do research, to write a publication or to teach a course, research, teaching and publication can be very individual activities. Idiosyncratic individuals should be encouraged, but too often are not. Their idiosyncrasies may challenge old ideas to produce new ones. Whilst supporting work may be divided amongst several research assistants, the academic product, that is the formation of ideas, is necessarily the product of individual minds. Ideas are part of a person. Manufactured goods are not. Ideas are assembled in the mind. So the "academic assembly worker" and "the manager of ideas" have to be the same person. In this respect academics are necessarily their own manager because of the nature of their product.

The intrinsic individualism of academic work means there is a constant organisational conflict between the needs of the individual, or small unit, and the management of the institution as a whole. This conflict produces a tension which is also creative, because there are always forces for change and hence adaptation. That may surprise those readers who think of universities as ancient unchanging institutions. They have a misconception. Universities have survived because they have adapted. They have been able to adapt because they are managed by a constantly shifting balance of forces, not rigid management structures. It is this shifting balance that is subtle and where academic politics lie.

II.   Academic departments

In most institutions of higher education, apart from individuals, the basic unit is the academic department. Departments are the units to which most lecturers feel they belong. True, they belong to faculties, schools or other larger units too; but lecturers label themselves and each other as chemists, mathematicians, town planners, historians etc. according to their disciplines, and departments tend to be collections of staff with a common discipline. Collectively they have an authority with reference to teaching and research in their subject. As a result they have some autonomy which needs to be respected by higher levels of management. Consequently academic government has a consultative and federal character that is not typical of most areas of employment.

The balances of power are also complex within departments. Members of departments have different status according to their ranks (e.g. lecturer, senior lecturer, reader, professor) and different amounts of power according to their personalities, involvement, power of language and so on. The head of department has the most power. He or she will speak for his/her colleagues at meetings of wider groups such as faculty boards and senate. Accordingly the head of department is likely to be at the centre of a wheel of communications and will argue the departmental case at committees for resources such as finance and staffing. More than anyone, the head takes decisions on behalf of the department and, having probably achieved his/her ambition in the institution, is in a position to resist the demands of popularity when the need arises. The head will write references for staff and will be very influential in departmental promotions and appointments. Particularly if the head is a professor, he or she is likely to serve professional and academic organisations outside the institution and thereby be a member of a wider network of contacts. These contacts and experiences give more information to the head and strengthen personal influence in the department.

The duties of head of department can be onerous and time consuming and have become more so in recent years (See Table 13.7 in the next chapter). Whereas the job was once primarily a matter of academic leadership, the current emphasis on managerialism and devolution of budgets to a departmental level has changed the nature of what is required. It is not every high quality academic who can also be an effective departmental manager. Some look forward to the challenge; others regard a period of headship of department as a chore. This period can also eat into research time. For this reason it is often the case that the headship of a department will be for a limited term, perhaps three to five years. Also for this reason it is increasingly common for respected non-professors to be prevailed upon to assume the headship of their department.

III.   Faculties

Faculties and "schools" are groups of kindred subject departments, such as the arts, the social sciences, the natural sciences, engineering and medicine. Many students will take their main and subsidiary subjects from departments within a single faculty although this is becoming less the norm with an increase in modular degree studies. Some departments may be members of more than one faculty. For example, Geography and Psychology may be members of the social and natural science faculties and they might require different entry qualifications for students taking science and social science degrees.

In a typical university such regulations are laid down by the Senate on the recommendation of a faculty board presided over by a dean who is usually part-time, holding office for perhaps three years. At one time the dean would almost always have been a senior professor, but non-professorial deans are increasingly common, as are permanent and full-time ones.

Because, in higher education, the individual is a productive unit, a very large number of communication links are required between central management and each productive unit. That is a big problem often not appreciated by academics themselves. Faculty boards are intermediaries for communication. There being too many departments, central university committees are often composed of faculty representatives whose reports need to be relayed to individuals by departmental representatives on faculty boards.

Faculty boards also exercise quality controls on behalf of Senates. They can provide a wider yet informed view of the work of their constituent departments. They vet proposals to do with courses, including their content, methods and examinations. In particular they watch the comparability of courses claiming comparable standards.

IV.   Senates and Academic Boards

Structures and powers may differ between the senates of the old universities and the academic boards of the former polytechnics. In spite of these differences, senates and academic boards have in common that they are the senior academic committees of their institutions and are chaired by the institution's senior academic, namely, the Vice Chancellor, Director or Principal. To maintain academic standards it is their job to stipulate academic policies and procedures.

The range of issues senates and academic boards may consider is enormous. The agenda may include discussion of recent government reports, reviews of fees, internal promotions, regulations for degrees and diplomas, consideration for honorary degrees, reports of examiners, staff development, the terms and conditions of academic appointments, regulations on student residence, standards for student admissions, the provision of journals in the Library, laboratory safety, a programme of public lectures, the establishment of a science park or commercial company using academic consultants, reports from faculty boards, the Open Day and the provision of audio-visual aids, together with any number of matters that might not be regarded as academic at all, such as reports of the Buildings Committee, the Finance Committee and the problems of parking cars.

From this range of activities it will be clear that senates and academic boards often have many sub-committees which pre-digest issues before submission to senate.

V.   Council, Court or Board of Governors

It is often forgotten that universities are multi-million pound businesses which require skillful management of matters such as finance, buildings and personnel. For these matters, in addition to senates and academic boards, pre-1992 universities have a council (court in Scotland) which is the executive authority of the university. Post-1992 universities have a board of governors. These bodies are composed of a majority of non-university members who will have business experience or represent the interests of the local community. They are usually chaired, not by the Vice-Chancellor, but by a respected non-academic member.

The inclusion of non-academic matters on the agendas of senates, and to a lesser extent of academic boards, reflects an important fact. During the period of expansion from 1964-81 the power of academic staff steadily, but almost imperceptibly grew, whilst the influence of members of the community on university courts and councils waned. The numbers of junior lecturers on senates also grew and since 1968 there is usually some student representation. The period of stringency in the 1980s resulted in a swing back of power to Vice-Chancellors and university councils (courts in Scotland) and was explicitly recommended by the Jarratt Committee of 1985 (see Chapter 3).

It is also a reflection of the fact that university management has become a far more complex business. No longer for instance can academic planning take place in isolation from knowledge of financial and estates matters. As a consequence it is increasingly difficult to maintain the distinction between senate as an academic authority and council as the business authority. In any case such large businesses cannot be managed on an everyday basis by a committee. So in addition to the committee structure, there are administrative departments managing a whole range of university activities, not least, how the money comes and goes.

VI.   How the money comes and goes

Universities receive their funding from the Government, student fees, the research councils, research contracts and other income generating activities. Money from the Government comes via a higher education funding council. The council allocates money for teaching according to student numbers, and for research according to a three or four yearly assessment of the quality of research in each department. In recent years there have been two trends in higher education finance: government funding has declined which has forced institutions towards income generating activities; and students have been expected to pay a higher proportion of the costs of their education.

In 1995-96 the total income of higher education institutions was approximately £10.7 billion (an increase of 6.6% on the previous year). The income was made up as follows:

Student fees	23%	(£2.511bn)
Funding council grants	42%	(£4.452bn)
Research grants and contracts	14%	(£1.554bn)
Other non-governmental income	18%	(£1.932bn)
Endowment income	2%	(£0.263bn)

The above figures are for the system as a whole and there will be significant variations in the sources and level of income attracted by different institutions. For example, some institutions are more research active than others. They are therefore more likely to attract research income from industry, commerce and public corporations. They are also likely to benefit from the funding council's allocation of research money. Every three years or so the funding council establishes panels to assesses the quality of research in each subject area (see Chapter 11). The outcome of that exercise determines the amount of money allocated to the institution for research by the funding council for that subject.

Institutions have seen this method as pressurising them to improve their research output, and various strategies have been adopted to do that. However, the amount of money available for distribution on research criteria has not increased at the same rate as the improvement in gradings. As a result departments have had to run to stand still -

higher gradings have not necessarily led to more money, but failure to improve has almost inevitably led to reduced funding.

Funding for teaching is determined according to student numbers. During periods when the government wanted to expand student numbers, institutions were allowed to exceed their agreed numbers, but would receive only the student fees for the excess, not any additional grant from the funding council. This was seen as a way of achieving "efficiency gains". In the late 1980s and early 1990s institutions expanded so rapidly that government targets for student numbers were achieved sooner than the government anticipated. As a consequence the government imposed a period of consolidation for full-time undergraduate student numbers. During this period institutions which failed to achieve or significantly exceeded their student number targets were likely to receive financial penalties. The Dearing Committee thought the Government should respond to increased demand for higher education. It expected, and the Government accepts, that much of the increase will be below degree level.

The two main sources of income for teaching have been student fees (in most cases paid for undergraduate students by the local education authority) and an allocation from a funding council. Different categories of student have attracted different

Table 12.1   Sources of university income (percent).
* Includes supplement arising from the Research Assessment Exercise (RAE)
** Including sponsorship from research councils and government departments

	%	
Recurrent Income		
Funding Council (e.g.HEFC) grant*	42.0	
Home Full-time Student Fees	16.0	
Overseas Full-time Student Fees	4.0	
Part-time Course Fees	0.6	
Research, Training and other Support Grants	0.3	
Endowments, Donations and Subscriptions	1.1	
Computer Board Grants	0.7	
Other General Recurrent Income	13.3	
Total General Recurrent Income	**68.0**	
Research Grants and Contracts **	22.8	
Income for other Services Rendered	5.2	
Total Specific Income	**28.0**	
TOTAL Recurrent Income		**96.0**
Non-recurrent Exchequer Grants		
Equipment and Furniture	3.3	
Building Works	0.3	
Professional Fees	0.1	
Teaching Hospitals	0.3	
TOTAL Non-recurrent Income		**4.0**
TOTAL INCOME		**100.0**

Recurrent Expenditure	%	
Academic Departments		
Academic and Related Salaries	28	
Other Salaries and Wages	8	
Other Expenditure	4	
Total General Expenditure	**40**	
Research Grants and Contracts	16	
Other Services Rendered	4	
Total Specific Expenditure	**20**	
TOTAL Academic Departments		60
Central Services		
Library	4	
Central University Computer	2	
Other Services	2	
Total Academic Services	**8**	
Total General Educational Expenditure	2	
Total Administration and Central Services	5	
	7	
Maintenance		
Rates	3.6	
Heat, Light, Power, Water	2.8	
Repairs and Maintenance	4.0	
Cleaning and Custodial Services	2.4	
Telephones	0.7	
Other	1.5	
Total Maintenance and Running of Premises	**15**	
General recurrent expenditure		
Total Staff & Student Facilities & Amenities	2	
Total Pensions	1	
Total Capital Expenditure from Recurrent Income	1.5	
Other Recurrent Expenditure	1.0	
Total General recurrent expenditure	**5.5**	
		35.5
TOTAL RECURRENT EXPENDITURE		95.5
Non-recurrent Expenditure		
Equipment	4.0	
Furniture	0.4	
Other	0.1	
TOTAL NON-RECURRENT EXPENDITURE		**4.5**
TOTAL EXPENDITURE		100.00

Table 12.2   University expenditure.

amounts from the funding councils. For instance an undergraduate history student attracts less than a student of clinical medicine. Such differences reflect the costs when teaching different types of student. The principle adopted is that income differs between types of student rather than types of institution. Thus a history student attracts the same government funding wherever that student is studying. For the future the Government has accepted that a greater proportion of funding for higher education should be related to the number of students thus reflecting the importance of student choice. Mandatory local education awards for tuition will cease and students themselves will be expected to pay a higher proportion of the cost of their higher education.

Student fees and funding council grants make up about 65% of institutional income although the precise percentages will differ between institutions. Student fees will include fees from overseas students who have to pay the full cost of their education. (There is no direct government funding for non-EU students, though there could be indirectly through the British Council, the research councils and special agreements.). Research income includes research grants and contracts attracted either from government sources or from private industry and commerce. Other income is generated from residences and catering services both to staff and students and to the conference trade during vacations; from investment income; from patents and copyright; and from other income generating activities such as short courses and renting accommodation.

Therefore the sources of institutional income in percentage terms look something like Table 12.1.

The significance of these sources of income is that institutions have freedom as to how to spend their money. For instance, the research strength of a particular department may contribute to a certain level of research income from the funding council, but that income is part of a block grant which the funding council gives to the university as a whole. It is up to the institution as to how it spends that money. It can allocate funds according to which departments have "earned" the money or it could redistribute the money to expand or improve in other areas. The increasing use of formulae in the allocation of funds from the funding council to institutions has made it easier to determine which parts of the institution are the major "earners" and has put pressure on institutional managers to use formulae for internal distribution which reflect how money is attracted. The extent of the use of such formulae differs between institutions, however. Also differing between institutions is the extent of financial devolution. Some, particularly smaller, institutions will remain centrally driven, but in large institutions it is likely that "cost-centres" (perhaps departments or faculties) will be allocated an annual sum from which all expenditure (salary and non-salary items) will have to come. Devolution clearly increases the level of responsibility for academic managers such as deans and heads of department.

Whatever the level of devolution, however, there will be certain common elements of expenditure for each institution. Indeed there are high fixed costs, particularly salary costs, which make it difficult for institutions to react to sudden changes in government policy. In addition to salary costs there will be recurrent expenditure on the Library,

Computing Centre, other central services such as audio-visual aids and the Language Centre, the central administration, examinations, and the maintenance of buildings including the salaries of porters and security staff. A breakdown of expenditure in terms of percentages may look something like Table 12.2.

What is evident is that institutions of higher education can no longer survive solely on the current level of government grant. They are dependent upon income which they themselves generate. That has implications for the way in which they are managed and the relationship which they have with their environment. In particular it places pressure on staff to respond to market forces. Many people think that universities survive on grants from the Government and do not have to live with market forces like the worlds of commerce and industry. They do. The management of every industry is different from others in some respects arising from the nature of their business. Likewise the management of higher education has its own characteristics and problems

Further Reading

David Warner and David Palfreyman, (1996) Higher Education Management: The Key Elements. Society for Research into Higher Education and Open University Press.

13. What are Academics Really Like?

I. Some misleading impressions

It is quite common for members of the general public to think that academics come from professional families, were sent to fee-paying schools, showed academic brilliance throughout their school days, going on to Oxbridge where they all distinguished themselves with first class honours degrees, went straight from being a student to being a lecturer and have political views to the left of centre.

Whilst there is an element of truth in some of these assertions, as a general picture it is wholly misleading. When considering what academics are really like it is best to distinguish between staff in the pre-1992 universities and the 1992 universities - those in the former Public Sector Higher Education (PSHE see Chapter 4), who were mostly staff in the former polytechnics and colleges of education. On one survey, about 60% of pre-1992 university teachers had fathers whose occupation was classified as in social classes I and II, but the proportion in the former polytechnics is probably lower. About a fifth of pre-1992 university teachers had been to a public school and that is more than for the population as a whole, but two-thirds came from grammar and direct grant schools (before the abolition of the 11+ exam and the formation of comprehensive schools). The figures for staff in 1992 universities are not very different: around 15% from public schools and 70% from former grammar and direct grant schools.

Around 85% of pre-1992 university lecturers have never studied at Oxbridge. Around 20% have a London degree; while over half in the 1992 universities and more than a quarter in pre-1992 universities went to one of the "Older Civic Universities" described in Chapter 4. Unfortunately, even in the 1992 universities, the proportion of academic staff from the ex-CATs or with CNAA degrees is very small. The old pecking order still exists. To some extent this reflects the fact that Oxbridge, London, the Older Civics, Newer Civics and Post-War universities, in that order, attract students with high grades in school exams and award a greater number of first and upper second class degrees.

It is true that in the early 1960s just over half university staff had a first class degree, but the figure fell to 37% during the rapid expansion in the late 1960s and early 1970s.

In 1973 only 13% of staff who taught on degree courses in polytechnics had a first, and another 33% had an upper second class, degree. Over a third had a Master's degree and more than a fifth, a doctorate. I don't know a more recent survey, but these proportions are almost certainly higher in the 1992 universities now. By any criterion the academic quality of the former polytechnics continued to rise throughout their short history.

If 13% and 33% seem low, it should be remembered that at the time that most 1992 university teachers obtained their professional qualifications, there were no degrees awarded anywhere in many of the subjects they teach, particularly vocational subjects.

These comparisons with pre-1992 universities should therefore be viewed with care. The experience and professionalism of polytechnic staff in the 1970s was shown by the fact that over two-thirds had professional qualifications and 82% had degrees. Only 14% had come "straight from college". Furthermore 25% had qualifications in teaching compared with only 19% in pre-1992 universities. The same was true of the ex-CATs at a comparable stage in their development. In the former colleges of education the proportion with both academic and professional qualifications has always been higher.

So far as political leanings are concerned, judging from surveys published at the time of the 1992 and 1997 elections and another 20 years earlier, it would seem that academic voting habits swing with those for the rest of the country. There may be a tendency to the left, but there is reason to think that there was a greater proportion voting for the centre parties than in the country as a whole.

II.   The changing composition of British academe
1.   The changing age distribution
Until recently a typical academic was appointed around the age of 28. There were good reasons for this. By that age they had had time to complete their PhDs and had had three or four years in some other area of employment or had strengthened their grant earning credentials with post-doctoral research. At that age they are energetic, still relatively cheap to employ, which they wouldn't be 10 years later, and can still enthuse with some creative or original ideas they wish to research.

Since the post-Robbins expansion this pattern of recruitment was thought to have created a problem that would shortly have to be faced. Staff appointed to universities in the late 1960s were typically from the low birth rate during the war years of the 1940s or the late 1930s. Staff appointed to teach vocational subjects as part of the polytechnic expansion in the early 1970s usually had a few more years of professional experience, and were a bit older, say in their early 30s. Hence they, too, were from the same cohort born in the 1930s and early 1940s. This meant there has been a tremendous bunching in the age structure of academic staffs and an expected massive staff turnover with retirements at the age of 65 after the turn of the century.

Suddenly, it seems, all that has changed. With favourable early retirement packages, and financial pressures to research resulting from the Research Assessment Exercise (see Chapter 11), the employment structure of universities is being transformed. In 1998, only 2.7% of staff in pre-1992 universities were aged from 56 to 65. With steady recruitment and retirement the percentage should be more like 25%. Figures 13.1, 13.2 and Table 13.3 show the contrast between pre-1992 universities with their research aspirations and the 1992 universities, some of which still prefer to concentrate more on teaching. Pre-1992 universities have appointed 14,300 Research Assistants aged 30 or less, and another 6,500 aged 31-35, mostly on short-term contracts with external funding. The number has more than doubled in less than 10 years. The 1992 universities have a tenth of these numbers and spend their money on lecturerships. Fewer (2.5%) have done sufficient research to be awarded professorships compared with 10.5% in pre-1992 universities and many of those have been recruited from the

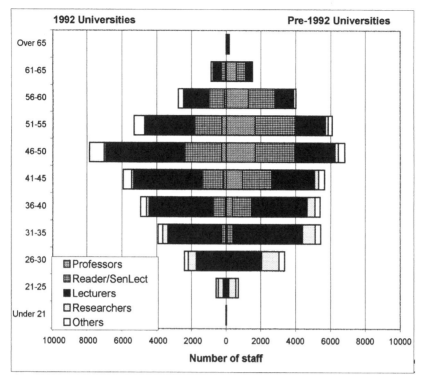

Figure 13.1   Age structure of staff wholly financed by universities, 1997.
Data supplied by the Society for Research into Higher Education, by agreement with the Higher Education
Statistics Agency.

pre-1992 universities. Lecturers in both kinds of university are now more likely to be
appointed in their 30s.

2.   Career prospects

What are the career prospects in universities for these thousands of Research
Assistants? They are not encouraging. You can see their numbers in Figure 13.2. Since
the 1981 cuts, nearly 20% of academic staff under the age of 30 leave in any given year
while the corresponding figure before 1981 was only 1%. Before 1981 many would have
become university lecturers with tenure until retirement age. In Figure 13.1 they can be
seen as a bulge now over the age of 40. Former Research Assistants must now seek jobs
elsewhere. The university lecturer scale is a long one with annual increments.
Consequently universities cannot afford to appoint young staff on permanent
contracts. Most of the best brains drain away after contracts of 3 to 5 years just when
their potential is coming into flower and they have learned enough to take further
responsibilities. The distribution in Table 13.3 also reflects patterns of promotion. Most
lecturers must wait until their 40s before they are promoted. Many don't get it even
then.

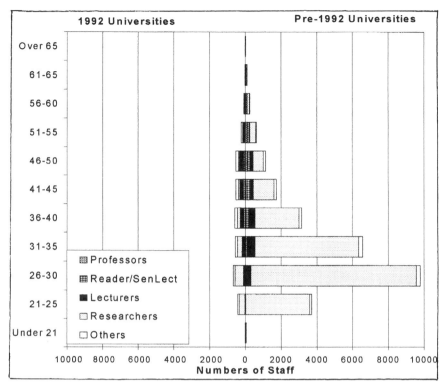

Figure 13.2 Age structure of staff not wholly financed by universities, 1997.

3.   How many part-timers are there?

Since the 1981 cuts the number of part-time academic staff has risen from 4% to over 10%. The proportion in the lower grades is slightly higher. The rise may herald a greater dependence on part-time staff which might also lead to a different style of relationships between students and their teachers. Much of the increase consisted of staff who retired early and then continued to do some part-time work to plug the gaps they left behind. What higher education needs is more part-time staff who work elsewhere and who have the strength of character to use that experience creatively to cross-fertilise perspectives and generate new lines of thought. But that doesn't easily happen because, as in any form of employment, part-timers are not influential because they have less time to spend in opinion forming groups.

4.   The poor but improving balance of female staff

There are too few women employed in universities and too few in senior positions. The table below shows the proportion of women employed as academics. It shows that the percentage at all levels is well below the proportion of men. It is also below the proportion of undergraduates. From student to professor men appear to be relatively favoured. Women are most prominent amongst the temporary jobs that are not university financed.

	Pre-1992 Universities		1992 universities		
	% Wholly Financed	% Not wholly Financed	% Wholly Financed	% Not wholly Financed	Total Number
Professors	9.9	0.6	2.5	0.1	7,965
Readers/Senior Lecturers	14.8	1.3	18.4	0.9	18,027
Lecturers	26.0	2.3	57.1	2.6	41,599
Research Assistants	4.9	35.2	4.0	3.6	29,548
Others	3.3	1.6	8.6	2.3	7,431
Totals %	59.0	41.0	90.6	9.4	
** Number**	39,177	27,182	34,620	3,590	104,579

Table 13.3   Percentage of staff by rank in 1992 and pre-1992 universities, 1997.
Data supplied by the Society for Research into Higher Education, by agreement with the Higher Education Statistics Agency.

However the scene is changing. Although there are no national statistics for Public Sector Higher Education before 1992, what evidence there is suggests the proportion of women appointed has increased at all levels where the posts have been wholly university financed. Indeed, so far as pre-1992 university financed staff are concerned, since 1978 at every level there has been a reduction in the *number* of men and an increase in the number of women.

The distribution of the sexes in academe is dominated by contrasts between disciplines. Table 13.5 shows that, with the exception of medical subjects, the division between humanities and sciences is clear. Thus former colleges of education have large numbers of female staff, while engineering departments have few. There are also wider variations within these cost centres. For example 6% of professors in biology are women; 2% in maths and computing; but only 0.5% in physics and chemistry. Overall the balance of the sexes is little different in 1992 universities from the pre-1992 universities.

Table 13.4   % of University staff who were women by rank and funding, 1997.
Percentages are rounded to the nearest whole number. Data supplied by the Society for Research into Higher Education, by agreement with the Higher Education Statistics Agency.

	Pre-1992 Universities		1992 universities		
	% Wholly Financed	% Not wholly Financed	% Wholly Financed	% Not wholly Financed	Total %
Professors	8	4	15	20	9
Readers/Senior Lecturers	15	50	24	50	20
Lecturers	29	40	37	53	34
Research Assistants	34	36	39	37	36
Others	87	43	30	41	38
Totals %	23	37	33	44	30
** Number**	9,097	9,742	11,427	1,571	31,837

	Wholly University Financed	Not wholly University Financed
Education	40	50
Language Literature and Area Studies	39	42
Medicine Dentistry and Health	39	45
Academic Services	38	43
Administrative, Business and Social Studies	28	43
Other Arts	27	35
Agriculture, Forestry and Veterinary Science	20	39
Architecture and Planning	15	29
Biological, Mathematical and Physical Sciences	14	27
Engineering and Technology	6	14

Table 13.5   Percentage of Full-time Academic Staff in all Higher Education Institutions who were Women, by Cost Centre and Source of Finance, 1997.
Source: Social Trends. Percentages are rounded to the nearest whole number.

5.   Ethnic minorities

Since their earliest foundations, universities have always welcomed students and scholars from other countries and ethnic groups. It is part of the liberal tradition and a willingness to seek the truth from whatever quarter it may come. So it's not just a matter of tolerance and mutual understanding; these things are matters of principle.

Look at the bottom two rows of Table 13.6. Generally speaking, the total number of academics in each ethnic group broadly corresponds with the proportion in the population as a whole. The Chinese and "Others" are over represented. Blacks, Indians and Other Asians are under represented, but not more than by half of one percent. The figures do not include clinical staffs in medical schools. They might increase the percentage of ethnic minorities.

Table 13.6   The percentage of ethnic groups in academic ranks, 1997.
Data supplied by the Society for Research into Higher Education, by agreement with the Higher Education Statistics Agency.

Ethnic Group / Rank	White	Black	Indian	Chinese	Other Asians	Others
Professors	97.4	0.2	0.7	0.2	0.3	1.1
Readers/Senior Lecturers	96.2	0.6	1.0	0.4	0.7	1.3
Lecturers	93.3	1.5	1.1	1.0	1.2	1.9
Researchers	87.3	1.1	2.0	4.8	2.2	2.5
Totals	92.7	1.1	1.3	1.8	1.2	1.9
Est. 1991 Census	94.5	1.6	1.5	0.3	1.5	0.5

Look a bit closer and you may have some reservations. White people seem slightly better at getting promotion, (though that's partly because ethnic minorities are younger). The number of researchers distorts the totals a little and, as we have seen, most of them have temporary contracts. So there's room for improvement. Nevertheless, compared with other areas of employment, universities' track record is favourable.

III.   Understanding how academics think

They think in different ways. But what ways? Academic staff think of themselves as physicists, engineers, historians, biologists, geographers, chemists and so on. They do not, in their work, primarily think of themselves as members of their university, or college. In everyday life it is loyalty to their group that is required, not loyalty to their wider institution. Where the subject group is large, their self-image becomes even more specific. They see themselves as physical or human geographers and organic or inorganic chemists. In a really large department they may split further so that amongst physical geographers, climatologists only have passing contact with geomorphologists.

The reason often given is that academics researching in a given field need to discuss their work with others who understand it. That may be true to a point, but in most institutions there could usefully be more cross departmental interaction on intellectual issues than there is. The crucial factor is one about human beings: they cannot run more than 6 or 7 close working relationships in any one environment and most people manage fewer than that. The same is true in factories or anywhere else.

Because group influence is so strong, academics working together develop certain common ways of thinking. For example, the marks of two examiners from the same department will correlate more highly than two in the same disciplines from different institutions. They make the same kinds of judgements because they tend to think along the same lines. They ask themselves the same kinds of questions and tend to use the same kinds of explanation. They have to, or they wouldn't understand each other.

But in reality lots of things can be explained in many different ways. A given question is capable of different kinds of answer, all of which are correct in their own terms. So in selecting one kind of explanation academics neglect others.

If I give a lot of examples you will see that each discipline uses several types of explanation. The study of literature includes understanding the author's intention, the function of language, the development of a plot, the morals and values involved, grammatical rules and an overall experience of a work. Biology is also concerned with function and development (of organisms, not novels, poems or plays). It also considers the spatial arrangement of anatomical structures, cause and effect, and the mathematical laws of inheritance. But morals, intentions and experience are seen as being too subjective for science. Physics, too, is strong on cause and effect, spatial structures and mathematical rules. Philosophers use logical (not just mathematical) rules and their experience. Economists explain the cost of goods as a function of supply and demand. They use mathematical rules to do it. Sociologists also talk about the functions of marriage. Psychologists explain behaviour in terms of intentions (motivation), child development, experience, biological functions, the structure of the brain and so on. This list could be lengthened.

The point is that there are certain types of explanation that are used across many disciplines. They explain in terms of spatial structure, developments over time, rules or "laws", cause and effect, functional relationships, intentions (purposes), values (including moral values), and personal experience. These overlap. Any academic uses several types of explanation whilst having preferences (which may be unconscious). Academics in the same small group will explain things in the same way. Few disciplines use all types of explanation, and most will reject some types as inappropriate. Disciplines can make sudden big advances by looking at new kinds of explanation (e.g. the study of human intentions to explain geographical facts) or by rejecting old ones (e.g. spiritual revelation and astrology).

This is a very brief account of the ways different academics think. As it requires the reader to look down, god-like, upon the thought patterns of some of the nation's best intellects, he or she may find that it requires re-reading and a lot of thought.

It can also be used by parents to appreciate their children's intellectual development in higher education. When students go to university they are trained to understand things in some ways more than in others. In short they get particular perspectives on life. The perspectives may be different from those of their parents. Higher education for one member of a family is an opportunity for all to widen their horizons. Unfortunately in practice, different perspectives often lead to interpersonal barriers, rather than opening new vistas.

IV. Academic life – what's it like?
1. How academics spend their time

What do academics do? They don't, as depicted on television, spend their time drinking port after lunch. Academics undertake research, teaching and management. Some do more of one than another, but in pre-1992 universities the overall ratios have long supposed to be around 40:40:20. The Dearing Report suggests that lecturers do spend about 20% of their time on administration, but professors spend 35%. Lecturers spend more than half their time teaching (if you include examining and guiding students as teaching duties). As a result research time is squeezed and those in pre-1992 universities complain about that. Even staff on temporary research contracts find they spend more than 40% of their time teaching whilst professors average less than 30%. Professors and heads of departments have such miscellaneous duties that they *average* little more than 10 hours a week on research. (See Table 13.7. Although the source is American, the duties are equally applicable in UK.)

One survey found that pre-1992 university lecturers worked an average of 50.5 hours per week, with senior lecturers working 2, and professors 4, more. Another report suggested 42 hours per week with rather less spent on research than teaching. Staff in the former polytechnics averaged 35 hours per week, with only 3 hours on research, but they need to work more than that now. In the Central Institutions of Scotland 35 hours a week on matters to do with teaching is a notional norm. (This includes time for marking, preparation and so on, but the notion of a 'norm' is a governmental fiction.) Research time has to be additional. A more recent study shows lecturers, senior lecturers and professors working 53, 54 and 62 hours per week respectively. They worked about 3 hours less per week in vacations.

2.   Academic stress

When the average academic is working over 50 hours per week it is not hard to see that when there is a significant increase in workload, something will have to give. It may be the quality of work or that some tasks are not done. More significant in the long run is the academics' feeling that they are no longer in control. Reputation, not money, is what motivates academics. They value freedom in the way they work. In the past academics have worked long hours and accepted lower salaries than they could get elsewhere because they felt they at least chose to do much of what they did. When this compensating feature is lost, morale plummets, motivation goes, despair sets in, essential relationships show friction, the quality of work suffers and ill-health results. In one Edinburgh college an investigation under the Health and Safety at Work Act revealed that doctors of 67% of the staff had diagnosed work stress as the cause of ill-health.

The increase in workload first occurred after the 1981 cuts. Where the axe fell in each university had to be decided centrally. So power went away from academics to university administrators. This trend has continued with the Jarratt Report (see Chapter 4), pressures for entreprenneurial activities, financial penalties and rewards for research performance, the assessment of teaching (see Chapter 11), the dramatic increase in student numbers and so on, each of these steps and more, creating ever greater stress.

Whilst the contract when accepting students applications is to award a degree normally 3 years later, the financial cuts and the decisions to close or merge departments are relatively immediate, the legal position is impossible. One report shows that the pursuit of research grants is now so competitive that eminent researchers, after spending 50 hours preparing an application may have it rejected as "not up to standard". The resulting deflation of morale made some give up altogether.

More serious for the nation, to preserve staff-student ratios and some morale many universities reduced student intake. Consequently they received fewer fees and block grants so that they could not support pump priming initiatives as the basis of applications for research funding. When the Government took such initiatives it effectively took control of what questions are researched. This not only meant a loss of university independence vital to a democracy, it meant that research became policy driven. It meant less freedom to pursue the truth unhindered. (See Chapter 10.)

I said at the beginning of this section that if you keep on increasing the workloads of academic staff, eventually something has to give. That 'something' is likely to be quality. But the quality of British research and higher education is the foundation of its reputation. To allay this, we have seen in Chapter 11 that methods to evaluate staff have been introduced at every level. But those methods increase workloads yet further and impose yet further stress.

V.   Staff Development in Higher Education

One way to reduce stress and maintain, if not improve, quality lies in staff development. University administrators have long had a well developed series of staff

Govern the department	
Advocate for the dept to central administration	Establish departmental committees
Set up and implement department plans and goals in collaboration with staff	
Prepare the dept for internal and external evaluation	Conduct departmental meetings

Manage teaching	
Timetable and assign teaching	Manage off-campus programmes
Supervise and schedule exams	Manage space and teaching budgets
Ensure departmental curricula are vigorous and up to date	

Manage personnel	
Select and recruit staff (with central administration)	Supervise staff promotion procedures
Initiate and manage staff development	Evaluate staff performance
Deal with unsatisfactory performance	Participate in grievance procedures
Inform and consult staff over departmental and university matters	
Prevent and resolve conflicts	Promote equal opportunities
Ensure compliance with legislation (eg health and safety)	Assign responsibilities

Promote departmental development and creativity	
Foster good teaching	Represent staff at professional meetings
Assist planning professional development	Stimulate research and publication
Encourage professional activities	Foster inter-departmental collaboration

Work with students and student issues	
Recruit, select, advise, counsel and assess students	Manage appeals
Encourage students to take part in departmental activities	
Monitor student evaluations of teaching	Monitor pastoral care
Liaise with student representatives, parents and employers	

Represent the department to the institution	
Interpret the discipline to the university	Build and maintain dept reputation
Represent departmental interests and requirements to the central administration	

Link with external groups	
Attend meetings of external groups (eg community, employers, funding agencies)	
Process departmental correspondence and requests for information	
Coordinate external activities	Ceremonial functions

Manage budget and resources	
Prepare, advocate and manage departmental budgets	Seek external funding
Promote staff entreprenneurial activities	Encourage grant proposals
Set priorities for conference and travel funds	Monitor consultancy work
Prepare annual reports	

Table 13.7   Head of Department's duties (Green and McDade 1991).

development opportunities through the work of the Association of University Administrators and its forerunners. University teaching, on the other hand, has been criticised for centuries, but until recently, in contrast to school teachers and university administrators, no training has been given. There is no point in evaluating academic staff and their departments if, having done so, there is no back-up service for improvements.

The Government's long-term aim is that all teachers in higher education shall require a professional qualification. It has welcomed the Institute for Learning and Teaching in Higher Education (ILT) which Dearing proposed should accredit university teacher training and to which full-time academic staff with teaching responsibilities should earn (junior or associate) membership status on completion of a recognised programme.

Arguably there has always been some staff development in research. This is the responsibility of heads of department. Departmental research seminars, conferences, the refereeing of research proposals by grant awarding bodies, and reading critical reviews of research are all activities where the highest standards are constantly being reasserted, often at a remarkable degree of detail.

1.   How staff development activities have grown

There has been resistance to staff development activities in the pre-1992 universities. The reason was not only that the need for staff development seemed to imply that senior staff had not been doing their job satisfactorily for many years, but that teaching essentially involves developing personal relationships. That is a very sensitive area in which to develop self awareness in the presence of one's colleagues, particularly for people who have hardly ever experienced serious failure. The privacy of the classroom had preserved teaching as a private matter. Senior staff feared exposure, but could not say so in case they seemed to be trying to hide a weakness. Now universities and their individual departments are being shamed into, if not required to, publish their staff development policies.

Staff development was better accepted in the polytechnics. Nearly all had appointed staff development officers, usually by some other name. The staff had a different attitude. This was partly because they had to justify the quality of their courses to the CNAA and partly because they had a heritage with closer links to industries where formalised staff training is normal. (It is not a coincidence that 5 of the 9 pre-1992 universities with full-time staff development units in the 1980s, were ex-CATs having the same heritage as the polytechnics.)

In spite of resistance in pre-1992 universities, it was during the 1970s that the methods of staff development which are now commonplace, were being explored and refined. Four broad strategies evolved, as follows. All four will be fostered by the ILT.

2.   Development by making staff better informed

One strategy is to do research into higher education and to disseminate information through the in-house publications or by whatever means is available. Academically, this is a respectable path. It includes using research methods to evaluate teaching an individual confidentially at his or her request. Research takes time. A lone staff developer cannot serve many staff by this strategy. And information alone, is slow to change attitudes. But in the long run this strategy is an essential component for staff development.

3. Staff development through conventional short courses

Another strategy is to run formal courses of a fairly conventional type with talks on specific topics, such as "student assessment", given by "experts", followed by discussion. Such courses are open to all and can serve large numbers if they care to come. The most common topics are small group teaching, lecturing, computer-based learning, personal tutoring, helping students to learn, assessment of students, research supervision and evaluating teaching. Unfortunately, with even quite small numbers, both the talks and the discussion tend to cover only general issues and rarely get to the heart of each individual's personal needs, unless a participant has the courage to raise them. Furthermore, merely talking about problems does not necessarily result in action, though arguably it is a necessary first step.

4. Developing attitudes and inter-personal awareness in support groups

A totally different style is analogous to co-counselling. The staff developer works initially with a small group of friendly colleagues developing close and trusted relationships. Ideally this might be a departmental group encouraged by its head. A supportive group provides members with confidence to express their concerns about teaching and in which to develop the self-awareness of inter-personal skills that is so important in teaching. Gradually the network of friendships widens and support in the institution grows. This approach, like the first one, is slow to bear fruit. It requires considerable inter-personal skill.

5. Training in skills

A fourth approach is to see teaching as a whole lot of skills from how to explain a concept to how to arrange the furniture for a discussion. Advocates of this approach developed workshop techniques in which participants practised various skills, were given feedback on their performance and then tried to perform them better. Video-recordings are a natural aid; and it is a short step from using the cameras in special workshop sessions, to taking them into the lecture theatre for thorough analysis afterwards, either privately, with the help of the staff developer, or in the presence of some of the students as well. Obviously this approach requires teachers to be able to face themselves, but once they have done so, their appreciation of the method is strong. To assist with particular skills the method is quick; but not all aspects of teaching can easily be analysed in terms of specifiable skills.

VI. Conclusion

Staff development, the age structures of staff, the short-term contracts of research staff and other topics covered in this chapter look towards the future. It is the future to which we must now turn.

Further Reading

National Committee of Enquiry into Higher Education (1997) Higher Education in the learning society (The Dearing Report) Report 3. Academic staff in higher education: their experiences and expectations. Batten E and Skinner M. (1997) The lecturer's job. A survey of conditions of service in new universities and colleges of higher education, commissioned by NATFHE the college lecturers' union. Crossbow research.

14. The Shape of Things to Come

I.   The inevitability of change

The fate of those who predict the future, be they Old Testament prophets or modern weather forecasters, does not encourage the practice. Nonetheless, it is an essential exercise to assist the plans and decisions of the providers of higher education and those thinking about participating in it as learners or employees. The world for which graduates are prepared is changing and will do so in major ways in their working careers and the rest of their lifetime. It may even change in the four to five years between thinking about course entry and emerging into the world of work, if they pursue full-time study. For those studying part-time, alongside work, the link between what they learn and what they do will be constantly under review, because jobs will be subject to constant change even within continuous employment. It used to be our choice whether we changed jobs. Now, and in future, our jobs will change whether we like it or not.

There will be changes, too, in the smaller world of higher education itself. The Dearing Committee, reporting in 1997, was supposed to develop proposals in the framework of a 20 year planning horizon. Disappointingly, it failed to have any vision beyond the immediate situation to which most of its recommendations referred.

This chapter tries to identify, briefly, some key developments in the wider world that should influence how higher education is planned and delivered. A longer section deals with the policy context of higher education, weaving the interlinked threads of four policy domains - access and participation, resources, curriculum, and structures and governance. A final section looks at choices facing those in charge of the system of provision and those looking to be provided for.

II.   The wider world

The world is getting smaller - or at least more accessible. We can now fly to Australia in the time it takes to drive from Land's End to John O'Groats. Think of how cuisine in Britain has changed because of holiday experiences in Europe that people want to repeat, or because of the inflow of people from the Commonwealth. So, the first theme here is of internationalism.

1.   Internationalism

The future graduate will work with people from many backgrounds so that language capability and cultural sensitivity may be two key expectations of employers. Even in any one country there is a variety of cultures and communities because of the movement of people. Even if we only speak English, we need to be aware of different kinds of English. The forms used by those who speak it as a second language are different from those who learned it as a child. Often they are more formal; their spoken language is closer to a written style. They may not share the cultural assumptions or knowledge on which metaphors are based, and cross-national humour is very difficult. US English, Caribbean English, Indian English are learned as first languages but are different from "standard" English and "received pronunciation".

2.   Availability of information

The international aspect of the world is part of the information revolution. This has two aspects: first, the explosion of knowledge and, second, the technology of processing and communicating data. Even today there is a big generation gap in attitudes towards video recorders, portable phones, computers, and the internet. Further developments may well leave the present younger generation behind their own children. Tomorrow's graduates must not only be IT literate, but have a base of competence and confidence in working with the technology so that they develop their capabilities in tune with new developments and interact with people technologically, virtually as well as internationally and interculturally.

For many professionals the development of knowledge will mean a need for constant updating - medicine with its allied fields is an obvious area, but law, following new legislation or new precedents by court judgements also needs constant renewal by practitioners. So do new techniques in design, or materials for construction, or EU requirements for accountancy, or research findings for social work or teaching. The professionalisation of sport and intense international competition has brought science and innovation even to arenas where amateurism used to be a quintessential element. Increasingly, chartered professional bodies will not renew a 'licence to practise' unless people demonstrate that they are pursuing continuing development activities.

3.   Demography

The third theme is a social one - demography. On average, the UK population is getting older - people are living longer and fewer children are being born than used to be the case. There are ups and downs of course but the trend is towards smaller families or childlessness: the latter a choice by up to 25% of women within 20 years according to recent forecasts. That has a number of consequences. For higher education the pool of young people from whom many entrants are drawn will be smaller, but there is some evidence that smaller cohorts will mean that there will be stronger encouragement by school staff for students to continue to study, after the age of 16. If early retirement remains as a norm, with longer life and shorter working life there is a pool of older people who may increasingly have expectations of higher education. Those who continue to learn actively live longer and healthier lives. The place of women in paid employment will continue to rise rapidly.

People are still moving out of the cities, in contrast to the last century, and are still moving from the North of England and Northern Ireland to other areas of the UK. This means that issues of the location of higher education provision will arise, and, here, national transport policy will be important - perhaps particularly for those older people just referred to.

4.   Economic and political decisions

There are economic issues related to this, and political decisions to be made. The proportion of GDP - our national wealth - spent on higher education was the same in 1996 as in 1976 even though there were more than twice as many students. The most difficult prediction to make is over politico-economic decisions. Will future governments see higher education as a cost or an investment for economic improvement, social equity and harmony, and cultural richness? Will education be more important in spending priorities than health, defence or a thousand and one other budgets? Within education, universities compete with other levels of provision - pre-school, primary, secondary, further, adult - and currently priorities are *not* in higher education. The immediate future looks no better. The best that may be expected is that increased spending on younger age learners will follow them up through the system to higher education as well as providing better prepared entrants because of the extra resources invested.

Currently, many employers spend little on training. Their belief is that the state or the student should pay for higher education. Where they have been involved in training, the state has often had to pay subsidies to them. Some of the larger, enlightened multi-national companies have shown that investment in the learning of the workforce improves productivity, absentee rates, days lost through disputes etc., but the contribution of education to organisational health remains generally under-recognised. It may be, within the EU (another political factor) that new requirements on employers will be introduced. That political frame of decision making may be a key future factor. If economic policy is to be agreed among 14 or more countries, is not an increased influence on education in member countries a logical next step, given the need for common standards for a mobile workforce to support the economy, and given the existing role of the EU in much social policy? The Maastricht Treaty in the early 1990s paved the way for that.

When an analysis like this is done more fully and rigorously it is called PEST – (covering **p**olitical, **e**conomic, **s**ocial and **t**echnological factors). These four factors often interact - the information technology revolution changes jobs (economic) and may create unemployment (social) as well as being a key to international communication (economic, political and social - think of satellite TV). In the next section there are also four factors, referred to as CARS - **c**urriculum, **a**ccess, **r**esources, **s**tructures. The two sets of factors should feature in the planning process of universities and colleges. Each of those institutions is required to produce and publish a strategic plan. So, if you want to compare their view of the future with what you read here, and study their intentions within that context - their *own* future - write to the Registrar and request a copy. Then, if you are looking to enter HE, decide if the future they envisage is one you want to be part of.

III.   The higher education world: policies and tendencies

1.   Fees as a resource

Policy and developments in higher education will continue to be driven by resources, much more than influenced by academics or even responsive to changing markets, though both those elements will continue to have some impact. The resource issue was the main factor in the remit of the Dearing Committee that reported in 1997. The first piece of legislation to follow from that, in 1998, had a title referring to 'teaching and learning' but was mainly about funding – fee levels, sponsorship for young people in employment, etc. Despite the commitments and safeguards in that Act, most people in higher education believe that fee levels will rise and that individuals will pay an increasing part of the cost of the courses they follow. Other beliefs are that government funding will not rise in line with further expansion so that unit costs funded from public money will continue to decline; and that top up fees *will* be introduced for popular courses and by elite institutions. For that reason, this section starts with resources and the issue will weave through treatment of access and participation, curriculum and structure and governance. The four factors are, anyway, interdependent: fee levels will affect participation levels and the structure and organisation of the curriculum will have to adapt to new patterns of participation.

The Dearing report recommended the introduction of fees for full-time undergraduates – part-time students and those on most other courses were already paying them. It also urged retention of grants. Government introduced fees, means-tested, but did not retain grants. On most other recommendations involving resources, the Government's Comprehensive Spending Review gave little more information, but did commit money to research and development (jointly with industrial foundations). There was a reduction in cuts planned by the previous government but still, given increased student numbers, there was a further squeeze on the unit of resource.

The immediate effect was a big drop in applications for full-time degrees from mature students – spouse income as well as parents' counts for means testing. The effect on applications from young people was negligible in the first year. It seems that higher education is seen by them as a 'prestige good' still worth investing in, even at a higher price. Research suggests that those with a degree earn over 10% more over a life-time than those with similar initial qualifications (such as A or H levels) but without a degree. Those pursuing degree level study part-time gain from the outset rather than losing out during study: once that finding becomes more widely known there may be a 'swing' to part-time study. Employer attitudes will be crucial and the influence of initiatives such as the University for Industry will be important in changing the culture of sponsorship of learning.

The link between fees and access was explicit in government statements – the extra income generated was to fund expansion. This was set at 500,000 extra students by 2002, later amended to embrace further as well as higher education. That target seems unreasonable but the commitment to growth by government, and to participation by young people is clearly articulated.

It is worth noting, however, that a growth in the number of graduates may reduce the salaries they can command and so change the earnings advantage a degree confers. That may affect the way people make their investment of study time so there is likely to be a shift to broken time study, and a continuation of the trend to study near to home. So more students will commute rather than be campus based. Postgraduate study 'end-on' to a first degree may also decline since graduates may prefer to pay off their loan debt rather than increasing it. The nature of campus life and of the 'typical' student experience will, then, shift, with the advantaged joining the fixed academic community and others staying within their 'home' community. The role of residential higher education as a 'rite de passage', a process of identity shift, even leaving home, will reduce, and the integration of the two communities be expressed through students. This will endorse the statements made often about 'town and gown' by university authorities who recognise that their surrounding area represents a resource. Similarly representatives of those cities and regions will see higher education institutions as sources of expertise and magnets to attract industries which want access to a knowledge and science based resource. Dearing stressed the importance of the regional base of most higher education and, in order to make effective use of resources, urged links with further education and collective strategic planning at regional level by institutions and other stakeholders.

Will fees continue? Will resource constraint also stay? In the medium term, yes; the longer term may be influenced by trends in access, and informed by experience elsewhere.

In Ireland fees were abolished in 1997 after a six-year experiment because they were seen to deter applicants from the lower socio-economic classes, the very group New Labour said it wished to help. Ireland had retained grants, too, even though small ones, so the deprivation of support was less than now proposed in the UK. The flow of students from the Republic to the north stopped in 1998. It may now reverse, as EU rules allow freedom of movement to study. Students from Belfast, studying in Eire, can therefore do so without payment. So, of course, can those from Bradford, Bedford and Bridge of Allen.

In the USA, during 1996-8, the Clinton administration increased federal funding for students and institutions by over 30% just as it was cut, again, in the UK. The home of capitalism and private higher education now gives higher levels of support to its system than the state based provision of the UK.

In Australia, the flat rate fee introduced some years ago has been replaced by three different levels related to the cost of courses. Those studying medicine or science now pay more than those following arts courses. The interest rate on loans has been increased and the threshold income level where repayment starts has been reduced. Students willing to pay the full cost of study, i.e. a higher fee, can be admitted over and above quotas agreed between a university and government agencies. No doubt the effect of this use of the fees and loans system as a regulatory mechanism affecting demand, and the admission of private students on a full cost basis will be closely monitored from the U.K.

When New Labour won the election, the UK re-joined UNESCO, which has a convention committing members to the 'progressive introduction of free higher education'. Do signatories on such conventions mean much, if anything?

There may be moves to 'harmonisation' within the European Union. Traditionally fees in most countries have been low or non-existent, but, recently the moves have been towards introducing or increasing them. The right of EU students studying in the UK to have fees paid by LEAs in the UK irritated the Tory government and may have been one unstated factor behind the 1997 policy.

2.   Other sources of income

What else in the future for resource policy? If we stay with fees it could well be that *tuition* fees will be protected by law but that fees for *services* could be introduced: for computing, library use, careers advice, and so on. Add-on fees might even extend to assessment (not strictly tuition) or handout material which may be collated and 'published' so it can be sold like a set book. Funding from HEFCE is now based on study credits. The flexible fee payment systems urged by government on institutions may mean that payment per module, rather than by year of study, will become normal.

If we move away from resource support to *individuals* and consider government resource for *institutions* the only future to plan on is for continuing parsimony. Three issues stand out. First, there is pressure for private funding, through loans or joint ventures, for capital expenditure, mainly buildings. In the first years of this Private Finance Initiative, there were few projects (the student village at the University of Greenwich was one) because it is difficult to see how investors get a return on, say, lecture theatres. Buildings are now designed, though, for multiple use – as theatres as well as lecture theatres, gallery and exhibition space as well as communal and dining space. Increasingly, not only is space jointly owned but services – catering, cleaning, payroll, major mailings – are contracted out so that university staff concentrate on their specialist functions where they are experts – teaching and research – and let other operate in their fields of expertise. The university as a collective consensual community, regulating itself, will contract away (in both senses) from control of some areas that are essential parts of the campus-based student experience.

Government expects more private money for research, to supplement static allocations from state funds. Medical foundations and charities, and drugs companies already give university medical schools and allied departments much more than does government through research councils. In some cases departments reach agreements about first rights of exploitation of inventions and patents by major sponsors. Such 'academic capitalism' will continue. It raises issues of scholastic independence and the ethics of association with some funding sources – cigarette companies, arms manufacturers – for institutions which, in the past, have claimed moral leadership or the right to act as the conscience of the state.

Pressure to generate income can risk putting prestige clients ahead of the core business (though less remunerative) of educating students and the disinterested pursuit of knowledge. The better quality buildings may be used for such prestige clients. Sponsored chairs can distort the curriculum profile, favouring commercial law over family law, for example.

The balancing factor to such institutional funding is that students now bring their own fees, and the associated government subsidy. That total market is still the biggest source of income for most places so that patterns of student choice, the profile of participation and rates of retention and return for later life (re)learning are important elements of the core business which will affect how such clients are treated, 'serviced'.

The change in fees arrangements may empower students to demand better quality; conversely, as in some USA institutions, it may lead to pressure for softer standards.

3.   Factors that might affect access

There are other factors that will affect access and participation besides money, though changes in student support may lead to more people studying part-time, or opting in and out of full-time study having 'earning' periods between 'learning' periods. Already many 'full-time' students work during term time, as they do in the USA and on the European mainland. This has meant that 'attendance' has become less demanded formally, provided that 'participation' is deemed satisfactory by the regular production of course work. Students are, then, learning, but some are being taught less – they become more autodidacts, self-taught, even though they are linked to a teaching institution. The library and computing-suite or 'learner support centres' are displacing the classroom. That trend will continue as more learning resources are made available for personal access. The role of the teacher must, then, change from being a simple transmitter of core knowledge to someone who, in a mass system, stretches the stronger students, supports the weaker ones and provides a core service to all students, helping them to frame knowledge and to approach it critically.

Modern technology will allow inputs from international sources. For example, USA universities are looking for bases in Europe and are supplementing a local campus with IT based programmes. Such 'colonisation' will continue as the higher education business competes in a global market. There may, then, be fewer overseas students in Britain, a trend that will be reinforced by problems in the Asian economies that started in the mid-1990s and will continue for some years. Few students will be able to afford to come on their own resources and governments will sponsor fewer. The quality of some outreach programmes from Britain working with overseas partners has caused concern so, again, there may well be a withdrawal process from physical presence and a removal of such outreach into the virtual domain. It seems likely that the shorter degree courses in the UK and the chance to improve their English will continue to attract students from an expanding European Community where a single currency will stabilise fluctuations in cost.

Among UK students we have already touched on a possible stratification, or reinforcement of current inequalities as the cost of study falls more on students and their families. Lower socio-economic groups may well be excluded, at least from full time study immediately after leaving school or college. The main change on campus may be in the growth in the proportion of students from ethnic minorities and women. The first will continue; the second may diminish. The age structure of minority communities is skewed towards the young so in each succeeding cohort their representation in the general population grows. In the main, they get better results at school and stay on at a higher rate. The support from the extended family tends to be stronger than among white Britons. As a result, in ten years' time, they could represent 25% of students, about twice the current level. This trend will be more noticeable in some places than others: in 1998 in at least two universities in London, the minority groups made up a majority of students whereas in, say, the two universities in Aberdeen or at the University of East Anglia in Norwich numbers were very low.

Women also perform better and stay on beyond the age of 16 more than men and, in 1998, were a majority of new students even though there are more men in any age cohort up to about 40. They have, though, been dominant among mature entrants and seem to have been harder hit by changes in funding. Their rise to equality, and more, may be slowed; but it will not be stopped. If there are to be role models for the students, the challenge of equality among staff members remains. For example, in veterinary science over 65% of students are women, but in 1999 there is not one female professor. As we saw in Table 13.4 on page ***, the average of women professors across all subjects is 9%; and among new appointments it has been barely 10% so change will come only slowly.

4.   Curriculum factors

Even if younger students are continuing to apply to enter higher education, their curriculum choice may be affected by economic calculations. The first figures after the introduction of fees showed rises in subjects such as software engineering, and marketing, and steep falls in teacher education, social work and some academic subjects in arts and social sciences. This suggests a continuing trend to a more calculated, instrumental approach to study choices and careers and, with more study from home with commuters and at home through computers, campus life may be more earnest and less exciting.

The anticipation of most staff is that, despite a more diverse student population through growth, demographic change, and, at last, a serious commitment by government to life-long learning, the curriculum offered in any one place will be less comprehensive. Subjects with small numbers will be cut out as managers concentrate on core, profitable, areas and strategic strengths. Within subjects, especially basic sciences, a core national curriculum will emerge even more than currently. There will be common learning resources shared among consortia of universities. This will be set in a common modular framework and outcomes judged against common national standards, as with school leaving qualifications and many vocational courses in FE. In Australia the idea that a standard test of "graduate level one skills" should be administered to all, is being discussed. The U.K could follow their example.

5.   Organisational structures

The Dearing Report, saw the need for a greater regional coordination of higher education provision and, if, regional structures are put in place, there could be collective strategic planning among institutions and across the HE/FE divide. Growth of higher education within further education colleges is being encouraged – in Scotland in 1998 over 20% of HE students were in such colleges – so more students in future will study in colleges with mixed provision. There may also be mergers of institutions: in some cities there is overlap of campuses of two or more universities. In others there is close proximity. In London, medical schools and hospitals have been 'rationalised' and higher education in general could well be the next service to be tackled, though several reports have shown that the benefits of mergers and system 'tidiness' rarely outweigh the problems involved, at least in the short term. Some FE/HE mergers have already taken place and more will follow as the structure of the system of provision moves to reflect the continuities involved in post-compulsory education and the need for collective planning to provide for learning through life as a norm for all citizens. The place of work-based learning and its recognition and academic accreditation is another key issue here.

The structures for research may well continue to separate from teaching. The essential link between research and teaching has been broken by separate assessment, separate funding and separate staff categories. There is, then, no reason for funding councils to support research in teaching institutions. Government gives as much money to private researchers as to universities, and a similar sum to its own research institutes separate from universities. One big change in the next decade, then, may be a move to a model used in some other European countries where academics have two contracts, one as a teacher in a university and a second as a researcher in an institute. The two organisations may be close geographically but controlled in two separate structures.

IV.   Conclusions and choices

Future gazing is fascinating. What this chapter has tried to do is give some insight into possible scenarios of provision early in 21st century. There is a need for change, some would urge radical change. We do not have a mass system of provision, but in David Robertson's phrase, 'A traditional élite system under pressure'.

When Robbins reported in 1963 most students were legally minors; now they are all adults. The 'ideal' size of a university was seen as 3000-5000 students; already several have nearly 30,000. Staff:student ratios were about 1:8, now they are twice that or more. The majority of students then were outside the university system; now most have been absorbed into an expanded system. So, we need to redefine what 'university' means and recognise that it has a diversity of forms and that higher education will still be pursued outside the recognised system – in further education, in work, and elsewhere.

What those leading and managing the system need to do is make choices, and balance conflicting interpretations and pressures such as:

• The conflict between diversity of provision and equity of access and participation
• Catering for the individual in a mass system
• The priority of quality and efficiency, with its impact on access. Do we go for ' nothing but the best, but not a lot of it', or 'something for everybody'?
• Coherence and continuity within courses or client choice within a common modular framework
• Local access to international provision
• A common fee or variation by cost, or pay by use

What those considering entry need is a clear statement of what is on offer and the conditions that apply from any specific provider. The contract between learner and providing agencies needs to be clear and comprehensive and overt, not the covert understandings and norms that may have prevailed hitherto. The academic community has been forced out of its closed cloisters. Students have become litigious and applied norms from the wider community within the autonomous institutional frameworks to enforce their rights, to get quality service, to insist on good practice. In future they will do so even more since they will be paying more of the cost. The challenge to develop and deliver is there for us all.

Index